ROUTLEDGE LIBRARY EDITIONS: THE ENGLISH LANGUAGE

Volume 16

STUDIES IN THE PHONOLOGY OF COLLOQUIAL ENGLISH

STUDIES IN THE PHONOLOGY OF COLLOQUIAL ENGLISH

K.R. LODGE

LONDON AND NEW YORK

First published in 1984

This edition first published in 2015
by Routledge
2 Park Square, Milton Park, Abingdon, Oxon OX14 4RN

and by Routledge
711 Third Avenue, New York, NY 10017

Routledge is an imprint of the Taylor & Francis Group, an informa business

© 1984 K.R. Lodge

All rights reserved. No part of this book may be reprinted or reproduced or utilised in any form or by any electronic, mechanical, or other means, now known or hereafter invented, including photocopying and recording, or in any information storage or retrieval system, without permission in writing from the publishers.

Trademark notice: Product or corporate names may be trademarks or registered trademarks, and are used only for identification and explanation without intent to infringe.

British Library Cataloguing in Publication Data
A catalogue record for this book is available from the British Library

ISBN: 978-1-138-92111-5 (Set)
ISBN: 978-1-315-68654-7 (Set) (ebk)
ISBN: 978-1-138-90966-3 (Volume 16) (hbk)
ISBN: 978-1-138-90968-7 (Volume 16) (pbk)
ISBN: 978-1-315-69385-9 (Volume 16) (ebk)

Publisher's Note
The publisher has gone to great lengths to ensure the quality of this reprint but points out that some imperfections in the original copies may be apparent.

Disclaimer
The publisher has made every effort to trace copyright holders and would welcome correspondence from those they have been unable to trace.

Studies in the Phonology of Colloquial English

K.R. LODGE

CROOM HELM
London & Sydney

©1984 K.R. Lodge
Croom Helm Ltd, Provident House, Burrell Row,
Beckenham, Kent BR3 1AT
Croom Helm Australia Pty Ltd, GPO Box 5097,
Sydney, NSW 2001, Australia

British Library Cataloguing in Publication Data

Lodge, Ken
   Studies in the phonology of colloquial
   English.
   1. English language – Conversations and
   phrase books
   2. English language – Slang
   I. Title
   427   PE3711
ISBN 0-7099-1631-0

Printed in Great Britain by
Biddles Ltd, Guildford, Surrey

CONTENTS

Acknowledgements	vii
Introduction	1
General conventions	26
Map	28
Chapter 1: Stockport	29
Chapter 2: Shepherd's Bush	51
Chapter 3: Peasmarsh	64
Chapter 4: Edinburgh	80
Chapter 5: Coventry	95
Chapter 6: Norwich	108
Chapter 7: Comparison and discussion	121
References	150
Index	155
Word Index	158

ACKNOWLEDGEMENTS

My grateful thanks are due to my nine anonymous informants, who agreed to be recorded; also to Sylvia Mann and Veronica Du Feu who assisted in two of the recordings. I would also like to thank Jacques Durand, Steve Pulman and Peter Trudgill for their helpful comments on and discussion of various parts of the book. The book would never have reached its final form, had it not been for the untiring and patient efforts of Moira Eagling, who typed the whole thing with great enthusiasm and consistency. Any faults in the end-product are nevertheless my responsibility. Finally, I am most grateful to Tim Hardwick, of Croom Helm, for keeping the book going in the right direction; I hope his patience is rewarded in this offering.

To Jackie

INTRODUCTION

This book has two main aims: one, to try to determine how best to account for both the differences and the similarities of phonological variation in British English within the general framework of native speaker competence; two, to establish a relatively small set of phonological processes to relate different styles of speech within one variety. To these ends I have investigated the speech of a small number of informants from disparate parts of Britain, varying in age and sex. This apparently haphazard choice of informants was determined by two considerations: geographical distance, to ensure that the speech would show up significant differences, and my ability to record informants in as natural a situation as possible, given the constraints of recording on tape. To make this most likely, I arranged recording sessions either with people who knew me well, or involved a good friend of my informant. The technique in the recording sessions was one of inducing natural conversation rather than using a question-and-answer interview structure.

Since I wanted to examine variation in English colloquial speech, the accents chosen were ones which, at least *prima facie*, were not in close contact with one another, and were drawn from different social backgrounds, both urban and rural. Since too my main interest is phonological, rather than sociolinguistic, I have not tried to give comprehensive pictures of the social stratification at each of my chosen localities (as is the case, for example, in Trudgill's study of Norwich, 1974). Nor is it my intention to present representative sketches of all possible varieties of English (as in the case of Wells, 1982). The spread of informants is simply to ensure variability in speech. Although I wish to stress the phonological aims of this book, I shall nonetheless consider certain problems of variety from a social point of view later in the Introduction.

The decision to investigate natural colloquial language also has two concerns underlying it. If linguists are attempting to establish a model of native speaker competence which is concerned with the regular patterns of speech, then it is only reasonable to test hypotheses on <u>all</u> regular patternings in <u>all</u> types of speech. The emphasis has for a long time been on word- and/or morpheme-based patterns (as exemplified by the pregenerative structuralists, e.g. Hockett, 1958, and Trager and Smith, 1951, and by the dominant TG approach of Chomsky and Halle, 1968), and even those interested in different tempi tend to use one- or two-word examples (e.g. Stampe, 1979). More thorough investigation of what Dressler (1975) calls "allegro rules" is necessary to add to the battery of word-based data already available. This book is a contribution to the presentation and discussion of conversation-based data in the expansion of the model of native speaker competence. It is for this reason, too, that I have presented extracts from my recorded material in fairly narrow transcription, so that any claims I make can be checked by the reader directly (given that my transcription is a reliable representation of the speech).

The second consideration follows from the first: do the phonological processes which are well described in the word-based analyses also occur in continuous conversation? Indeed, to put the question in a more extreme form, are word-boundaries relevant in rapid colloquial speech, where they quite clearly undergo considerable alteration (see, for example, Zwicky's brief discussion of Welsh, 1972)? We need to discover whether or not the phonological processes discernible in rapid speech are fundamentally different from those of slow, careful speech. The main difference may be that in slow speech any processes that occur are for the most part obligatory, whereas in rapid speech they are optional. For example, in all varieties of English *pleasure*, which, we will assume, has an underlying /-zj-/, undergoes a "palatalization" process so that it is pronounced with a medial [ʒ]. On the other hand, *as you* in rapid speech can be pronounced either [əz jə] or [əʒə], although the latter is more likely. This means that we shall have to differentiate between instances where a rule is applied obligatorily and instances where the same rule is applied optionally. This is a topic to which I shall return in the final chapter.

THE TERM "PHONOLOGY"

As can be seen from what has already been said, my general approach to phonology is "generative", that is to say, I am concerned with capturing (part of) the tacit knowledge of the various informants I have recorded with regard to their phonological systems. The knowledge of each idealized speaker/hearer is not necessarily represented by something that resembles formal standard spoken English. I shall discuss the details of the phonological component in the last chapter, when I try to formulate the processes in rule form, but some general considerations can usefully be dealt with here.

For the basic element of phonological description, I shall use the segment without entering into any discussion of other possible alternatives (e.g. the undoubted syntagmatic or "prosodic" nature of certain features of speech, as discussed by Lyons, 1962; Palmer, 1970; Hyman, 1975: 233-38; Goldsmith, 1976a & b; Libermann and Prince, 1977, and others); nor shall I pursue here the notion that segments can be hierarchically modelled, as proposed by dependency phonology (see Anderson and Jones, 1977; Anderson and Ewen, 1980; Ewen, 1980; Lodge, 1981; Anderson, ms). However, in the final chapter I shall consider certain phenomena which suggest that some form of non-linear approach to phonology is appropriate. Throughout the book I shall work with the notion of phonetically based phonological processes as a basic feature of phonological systems (cf. Stampe, 1979). I shall discuss the most common of these in British English in the next section.

Since my main interest is in the phonetically motivated processes, I shall not be concerned with the phonological aspects of morphological alternations of the *serene - serenity* or *electric - electricity* type (cf. Chomsky and Halle, 1968; Fudge, 1969b). However, since this is an important theoretical issue, a brief discussion of it is in order here. In the model proposed in SPE the lexical entries are all morphemes with a single specification of features from which all alternant surface realizations are derived by rules. (These lexical entries are also fully specified in terms of features at the systematic phonemic level, a point I shall return to in the final chapter.) A considerable amount of the argument in favour of this approach revolves round the Latinate vocabulary of English (*serene - serenity*, etc.), but words which enter into other alternations, such as *take - took*, and those which have no alternations, e.g. *fade*, are treated in the same way. Thus, *sane*, *take* and *fade* all have underlying /æ/ as their vowel in the lexical entries. There are two claims made by this approach which need particular

mention: one, that these vowel alternations are part
of a native English speaker's competence, and two,
they should be handled by phonological process rules.
The first claim is difficult to prove or disprove in
relation to all speakers of English. It is no doubt
true that educated people, who come into contact with
Latinate vocabulary a great deal, would consider
these alternations to be a productive part of their
linguistic system. If they came across a Latinate
word previously unknown to them, or were given a
made-up one, e.g. *oblatile*, they would be able to
provide the appropriate alternant(s), e.g. *oblatility*,
in this case with the alternation [aɪ] - [ɪ], as in
divine - *divinity*. However, it is much more difficult
to make claims of this sort for less sophisticated
speakers of English, who may well come across such
items of vocabulary only rarely. For them such words
do not form a substantial part of their lexicon, and
may have been learnt piecemeal([1]).

The second claim has been argued about since SPE,
and is related to the problem of abstractness of
phonological representations. Tiersma (1983) gives
a number of arguments against a solely morpheme-based
model of the lexicon. Although he uses rather more
straightforward material from Frisian, in that it can
be more easily demonstrated that the alternations in
question are non-productive and becoming fossilized,
his arguments can be applied to the Latinate vocabulary of English. One argument he puts forward is
that each member of the alternating pairs is distinctive elsewhere in the lexicon (1983: 71). This
certainly applies to the English forms too: *fade/fed*,
reed/red, *fine/fin*. However, since the biuniqueness
condition is demonstrably unhelpful in making phonological statements (cf. Hyman, 1975: 68-69 and 90-91),
this argument can only be used against identifying
all occurrences of an alternating pair with the same
underlying element, whether there are any alternations
or not. That is to say, the [ɪ] in the stressed
syllable of *divinity* can be derived from /aɪ/ because
of the alternation involved, but the [ɪ] of *fin* is a
distinct unit, /ɪ/. If the /aɪ/ of *fine* is associated
with that of *divinity*, there is still no loss of
distinction between the alternating and the non-alter-
nating types, because *fine* does not occur in contexts
where trisyllabic laxing can take place. As far as
English is concerned, the arguments against the SPE
treatment of such forms must be psychological, rather
than phonetic and distributional. Since this is
outside the scope of this book, I shall not pursue
it further, but an investigation of how children cope

with the acquisition of such alternations and tests of the sort outlined in footnote 1 would help to provide an answer (²). In terms of the interests and aims of this particular book, it is quite clear that the accents of English under discussion need all the underlying elements involved in the Latinate alternations (³), and that they are related morphologically in certain instances. Exactly how this should be incorporated into the grammar can be left for separate investigation.

In the phonological discussions I have avoided both the extreme positions of, on the one hand, abstractness (cf. Fudge, 1967, 1969a & 1969b; Trudgill, 1974), where the underlying elements have no phonetic values, and, on the other hand, concreteness (cf. Hooper, 1976), where abstraction of any kind from the surface data is severely restricted. (See Dresher, 1981, for discussion; see also Kiparsky, 1968.)

THE PHONOLOGICAL PROCESSES

I am assuming that English is subject to a number of widespread phonological processes. Many of these have been recurrent throughout its history and some have been continuing for a century or more. (It may share them with other languages, too, but that is not the concern of the present book; on linguistic processes in general, see Aitchison, 1981; on phonological processes, both synchronic and diachronic, see especially, Stampe, 1979, and Anderson and Ewen, 1980.) However, these processes are not distributed uniformly throughout the different accents of English, and I hope to show how the different distribution of the processes helps to distinguish between the different accents. For example, intervocalic voicing of voiceless stops is a widespread feature of English phonology: it is a recurrent feature of the Peasmarsh accent (see Chapter 3), but it is not found at all in the speech of the Stockport informants (see Chapter 1). Phonological processes are not obligatory but are normal, especially in the type of English under consideration, colloquial conversation. A process relates two or more alternant forms (which may occur in different styles, e.g. colloquial versus formal); if there is no alternation, then no process applies, as far as the synchronic system is concerned. For example, in colloquial RP consonantal harmony and cluster simplification apply to nasal + alveolar stop + C sequences as in *sand-castle*. These forms are related to the careful, formal style of pronunciation, giving three possible pronunciations:

5

[sandkɑsl], [saŋgkɑsl] and [saŋkɑsl]. On the other
hand, with a word such as *handkerchief* no such alternant pronunciations exist: [haŋkətʃijf] is the only
one possible. In this case the process does not
apply, even though from a diachronic point of view
it did at some earlier period. Consequently, for
this word there is no underlying form: */handkətʃijf/.
The same applies *mutatis mutandis* to the /t/ in, on
the one hand, the variant pronunciations of *last news*
with and without a [t], and, on the other, words such
as *listen* and *glisten* with no alternative pronunciations.

I shall give a general description of the most
common processes here, and give further details in
the individual chapters, where I shall also introduce
a few minor ones as necessary. In the final chapter
I shall give formalized versions of the rules involved.

(i) *Lenition*

The general nature of lenition is discussed by Hyman
(1975: 164-69), Hooper (1976), Foley (1970), and
Anderson and Jones (1977), all from somewhat different
points of view. Anderson and Ewen (1980: 28) present
the following schema, which I have adapted here by
using traditional articulatory categories:

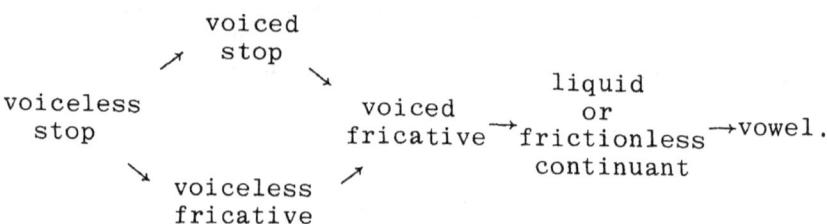

The direction of lenition is from left to right; a
sound undergoing lenition will not necessarily go
through the whole process; that is, a voiceless stop
may become a voiced stop and go no further, as in
Peasmarsh [bɑdm̩] *bottom* (line 18), or a sound further
along the chain, not itself a product of lenition,
may be subject to the next step of the process, as
when a liquid becomes a vowel in Shepherd's Bush
[ɒtɑɪʉ] *style* (line 5). Voiceless stops may become
voiced stops, as in the Peasmarsh example above, or
they may become voiceless fricatives, as in Stockport
[peɪɸo] *people* (line 13). The usual environment for
lenition to take place is intervocalically.

(ii) *Harmony*
This is a more general term than the usual one, "assimilation". Certain features of two or more segments, either consonantal or vocalic, harmonize, i.e. are the same in each segment. This can apply to both contiguous and non-contiguous segments (see Stampe, 1979: 76, and Lodge, 1983, for a discussion of this phenomenon with reference to child language as well). Vowel harmony is well exemplified by Turkish (Lyons, 1962, and Hyman, 1975: 182), but does not occur in the varieties of English presented here. Consonantal harmony, of which there are several types in British English, is usually called assimilation and not given the same phonological status as vowel harmony (cf. Gimson's discussion of English, 1962: 270-73), or it is applied to child language (cf. Vihman, 1978). (There are also suggestions that vowels in VCV structures harmonize generally; see Hardcastle, 1981: 55-56.) However, there is no reason to assume that any of these types of harmony are not basically the same phenomenon from a phonetic point of view. They can all come under the general heading of ease of articulation and seem to serve the same purpose. Whether segments intervene between the two harmonized segments or not, does not make any difference. In fact, Stampe (1979: 76) claims that there is no such thing as non-contiguous harmony, since the features in question continue through the intervening segments as well (cf. also Lodge, 1983, for a discussion of retroflexion in one instance of *somebody* as pronounced by a 3¾-year-old Stockport boy).

The features that harmonize may be manner of articulation, place of articulation, voice, tongue height; in fact, any feature can harmonize. The most common instances of harmony in English are those of place, e.g.

[tɛm menePˀ] *ten-minute* Stockport (18)

[kˈɑːmp bɪ] *can't be* Shepherd's Bush (27)

[əm bæk] *and back* Peasmarsh (52),

the most widespread applying to the underlying alveolars and dentals, even in RP (cf. Gimson, loc. cit.). The syllabic alveolar nasal harmonizes, sometimes to the preceding consonant, sometimes to the following one, e.g.

[ʊɛkŋ̊̊] *reckon* Stockport (17)

[ɐplekˈɛɛʃŋ̊ fɑm] *application form* Stockport (9).

7

The so-called velars, /k/ and /g/, harmonize with the following vowel, giving a range of realizations from palatal to velar, and even uvular for some speakers before [ɔ:]-type vowels. I have not indicated this in the transcriptions, as it applies to all the accents under consideration (and probably all accents of English). The labials can also harmonize, but the range is only bilabial to labiodental. This is most common in the one Stockport informant, Y, e.g.

[geβ me] *give me* (9).

Another common harmony of place in English is what we might call palatalization, that is the change of /t d s z/ to a palato-alveolar in front of /j/, e.g.

[ɔ:wɪʒ jɷus] *always used* Shepherd's Bush (1)

[pɹæpʃ jɷud] *perhaps you'd* Peasmarsh (53).

This is a process which has been going on for some considerable time in all types of English; some words have finished the process, as witnessed by those words with only one pronunciation with a palatal articulation, e.g. *nature, sugar*; others show fluctuation between two possible pronunciations, e.g. *issue* with [-sj-] or [-ʃ-]. (Note that a few words have avoided the process by dropping the palatal articulation; these words have alternative pronunciations with a non-harmonized alveolar followed by the palatal, or with no palatal at all, e.g. *suit* with [sj-] or [s-].) For the purposes of this book I am particularly interested in those cases where there are environmentally conditioned variants, in particular across word-boundaries.

Harmony of manner is less frequent, but applies most commonly to /ð/. In some speakers it applies to other sounds as well. E.g.

[an̪ n̪ə] *on the* Stockport (26)

[wɛɫ lɪ] *Well the* Shepherd's Bush (7)

[ɪn̪ n̪æʔ] *in that* Peasmarsh (34)

[ə̃j̃ jə] *and you're* Stockport (25) (+ place harmony)

[dʒaβ ð̃ɛ̃] *job then* Stockport (6)

[dɛʊ ʋof] *dead rough* Stockport (62) (+ place harmony)

In the case of /ð/ the harmony is left-to-right, rather than the more usual right-to-left.

Voice harmony is, of course, well known in English morphology, as in the formation of noun plurals, the 3rd person singular of the general tense and the past tense, and in this all the accents under discussion are alike. Otherwise, it is only sporadic, as in

[pɛɪvmənᵈ] *pavement* Shepherd's Bush (28).

(It is also found in West Yorkshire speakers, as in [bratfəd] *Bradford*, cf. Hughes and Trudgill, 1979: 58; Wells, 1982: 367.) We may note here that one of the alternative first stages of lenition could be interpreted as voice harmony, that is between two voiced sounds the voicing continues through what would otherwise be a voiceless stop, as in

[bəd ɪts] *but it's* Peasmarsh (18)

[bɑdm̩] *bottom* Peasmarsh (13)

[dæɷn də] *down to* Peasmarsh (16).

(iii) *Consonant cluster simplification (CCS)*
In many contexts three (or more) consonants in series are reduced in number. The deleted consonants are usually stops (oral and nasal), though other sounds are also sometimes involved, details of which I shall give in the individual chapters. Consider the following examples:

[ʔtʃɛendʒ ü̥e] *changed my* Stockport (31)

[kɛπ ɱe] *kept my* Stockport (57) (+ labiodental harmony)

[mʌɷs weɪkes lek⁺] *most weakest little* Stockport (62)

[fæɷn nɛm] *found them* Stockport (75)

[spo:s ʔ beɪ] *supposed to be* Stockport (85)

[sɛɸ̃ ʔaʔ] *except that* Stockport (2)

[dʒos stɑk] *just stock* Stockport (21)

[dʒos ʋaeʔ] *just right* Stockport (23)

[seɪm tə] *seemed to* Stockport (48)

[dʒʌs kɷdn̩ʔ] *just couldn't* Shepherd's Bush (4)

[sɪim tə] *seemed to* Shepherd's Bush (8)

[ən̪ n̪æʔs] *and that's* Shepherd's Bush (15)

[lɷʔ sʌmθɪŋʔ] *looked something* Shepherd's Bush (48)

[paɷnz daɷn] *pounds down* Shepherd's Bush (51)

[nɛks wɪik] *next week* Shepherd's Bush (55)

[feɪs weɪ⁺d] *First World* Peasmarsh (25)

[dʒes lɛf tə] *just left to* Peasmarsh (38)

[ʌʊɫ mæːn] *old man* Peasmarsh (40)

[spɛʃɫess] *specialists* Stockport (77)

[fɹɛnz̥] *friends* Edinburgh (91).

All the above are examples of /t/ and /d/ in the context: C__+C, where + = morpheme boundary, and the first consonant has the same voice feature as /t/ or /d/ (⁴). This means that /t/ after voiced sounds is not deleted. /k/ is also deleted under the same conditions, e.g. [aːst] *asked* Coventry (69). (/p/ may do, as well, but there are no examples in the recorded material, cf. Lodge, 1981: 35.)

The nasal /n/ is treated differently according to the following sound and from locality to locality. For example, in Stockport it is either deleted completely or the alveolar contact is deleted leaving nasality in the preceding vowel phase, when the following sound is /t/ ([ʔ]), e.g.

[wɑʔ] *want* (54)

[wʌ̃ʔ] *won't* (61) x 2.

On the other hand, with /d/ following, /n/ is not deleted, but the /d/ is, in accordance with the above examples, e.g.

[fæʊn nɛm] *found them* (75).

In Shepherd's Bush and Peasmarsh, however, /t/ is often deleted <u>after</u> /n/, when a vowel follows, e.g.

[dɪdn̩ ʌndəstæːmb] *didn't understand* Shepherd's Bush (39)

[kaˑn ɹivn̩] *can't even* Peasmarsh (11).

Details of such differences from locality to locality will be given in the separate chapters. (For a detailed discussion of CCS in Stockport within a dependency framework, see Lodge, 1981.)

There is a special case of deletion of /d/, /v/ and /z/ in the auxiliary verb forms, such as *wouldn't, haven't, doesn't* (cf. Petyt, 1978), which applies to a large number of English accents, and is specific to this class of verb. I do not intend to deal with this in detail here, but clearly the conditions for the deletion are not those of CCS.

(iv) *Unstressed vowel deletion (UVD)*
Another widespread feature of colloquial English is the deletion of unstressed vowels, either completely or by reduction to a glide. The commonest examples of this, which applies to RP as well, are the so-called weak forms of the auxiliary verbs, such as

I've, he's, we're. I shall not be concerned with such forms in the individual localities, as they occur in all of them. However, it is worth noting that Zwicky (1972: 610-11) relates some of the auxiliary contractions to a syntactic constraint, distinguishing between "dependent" and "independent" auxiliaries. The former, including *will, are* and *am*, cannot contract unless they are in close syntactic relation with the preceding word. Although this is not the place to consider this in detail, in many accents *will* is independent rather than dependent, e.g.

> There's a man lives next door'll mend your fridge for you

is perfectly normal in Stockport. (See Lodge, 1979, for a discussion of similar constructions in Stockport.) The contracted negative /nt/ is also discussed by Zwicky (1972: 612-13) and he suggests that it enters the phonological component in that form. (Hasegawa, 1979: 136-37 suggests that such contractions should be handled in the lexicon.)

The details of other types of UVD, which are phonological processes, are locally varied and will be given in each chapter. One of the commonest forms of this process is the deletion of the first [ə] in syllable sequences (regardless of word boundaries), whose "full" rhythmic pattern is CV́CəCV̆, where C = at least one consonant, as in *labourer* and *comfortable*. E.g.

> [əpʌɔɫstʊə] *upholsterer* Stockport (37)
>
> [ɹɪmɛmbɹ əm] *remember them* Peasmarsh (35)
>
> [batɹe] *battery* Stockport (79).

The resultant cluster must be a possible English one or the deletion cannot take place, e.g.

> *[hʌmblɹ ən] *humbler and*.

An example of the reduction to a glide is:

> [ðj ɐdmɪnɪstɹeʃn̩] *the administration* Edinburgh (29-30).

A different environment in which an unstressed vowel is sometimes deleted is where two consecutive vowels come at a word-boundary: V # V. In such cases only one vowel remains, e.g.

> [ʃɛeʔʃe baœʔ] *shakes you about* Stockport (49).

11

(v) *Linking r and rhoticism*
The insertion of r between two vowels belonging to different syllables is a widespread linking device in English. The circumstances under which it is used vary considerably from one area to another, and even from one speaker to another. Even those speakers who use it widely do not always use it. The following pairs of examples are by the same informant:

    [fəʊ ɛedʒez] *for ages* Y, Stockport (57)

    [ɛːdʊɛsə op] *hairdresser up* Y, Stockport (56)

    [endoəɹ ɛːɹeəl] *indoor aerial* N, Stockport (67)

    [jə ɔːnnɹe] *your ordinary* N, Stockport (77)

    [heə ən] *hair and* Shepherd's Bush (2)

    [pʻɛɪpəɹ a̱] *paper I* Shepherd's Bush (3).

In accents with post-vocalic r the situation is somewhat different, since in a great many instances, e.g. the six given above, the words end in /r/ anyway. In such accents the variety of r used may be used as a link between words where there is no final /r/, e.g. *law of*, or the glottal stop may be used, e.g.

    [ðə ʔæɒs] *the house* Peasmarsh (38).

(For words such as *comma* and *china* in rhotic accents, see Wells, 1982: 221-22.)

    The status of /r/ is somewhat complicated in English in that its incidence varies from one accent to another. The difference between rhotic and non-rhotic accents is in the occurrence or not of /r/ before a consonant. Thus, non-rhotic accents have no alternating forms of words such as *farm*, *port*, *church* and *perplex*, so such words have no underlying /r/, as they do in rhotic accents. This reflects the inability of non-rhotic speakers to predict correctly the occurrence of word-internal, preconsonantal /r/. (On this point, see Trudgill, 1980/83: esp. 148-49.) On the other hand, word-final /r/, which is retained before vowels even in non-rhotic accents, does involve alternations, so that /r/ can be postulated in the underlying forms of such words as *car*, *door*, *fur* and *letter*. In the case of unstressed -*er* the underlying form is syllabic: /r̩/, which may lose its syllabicity by means of UVD. We need an /r/-deletion rule to account for its non-occurrence before consonants, and the following realization rules for /r/:

$$/r/ \longrightarrow [ə] / \underline{} \begin{Bmatrix} C \\ \emptyset \end{Bmatrix}$$

$$\longrightarrow [əɹ] / \underline{} \begin{Bmatrix} V \\ r \end{Bmatrix}$$

$$/r/ \longrightarrow \emptyset / \underline{} \begin{Bmatrix} C \\ \emptyset \end{Bmatrix}$$

Then there is /r/-insertion in those cases without underlying final /r/ for those people who have forms such as [lɔɹ əv] *law of* (for numerous examples, see Wells, 1982: 223-25).

An alternative solution is not to postulate any underlying /r/ in word-final position either and simply have an /r/-insertion rule (cf. Wells, 1982: 222). However, the advantages of the former solution are (i) rhotic and non-rhotic accents have the same underlying forms in respect of final /r/, and (ii) it accounts for the fact that *soaring* has an /r/ but *sawing* does not for many speakers (cf. Wells, 1982: 225). Those who do have an r-sound in *sawing* etc. have extended the application of /r/-insertion, not differentiating between word-final and word-internal /ɔ/. There are even further extensions of /r/-insertion in some accents, e.g.

[jəɾ ɛniθiɡ̃] *you anything* Coventry (3)

[bəɹ a:ʔ] *by heart* Norwich (32).

(Cf. [t'əɹ ëiʔ] *to eat*, Trudgill, 1974: 162; also Wells, 1982: 227. For some speakers in Norfolk even the indefinite article has linking /r/, e.g. [əɹæpɫ] *a apple*.) Finally, we must note another type of speaker, who has no linking /r/ at all except word-internally, as in *nearest*, and uses [ʔ] instead. For them no underlying final /r/ is necessary.

To sum up, there are basically three types of speaker with regard to underlying /r/:
    (i)   Those with preconsonantal /r/ (rhotic);
    (ii) Those with word-final /r/ and /r/-deletion;
    (iii) Those without syllable-final /r/ and /r/-insertion.

/r/-insertion applies in different degrees for (i) and (ii), but for all three types the rule has the same phonetic formulation: any vowel lower than mid, i.e. [ə] and lower, whether long or short, stressed or unstressed, allows linking /r/ to follow before another vowel. For speakers of type (iii), /ə/ not /r̩/ appears in the underlying forms of *letter* etc. There are also some speakers of type (ii) who delete /r/ intervocalically, as in [veɪ] *very*, giving the same output as (iii) for words ending in /r/ before a vowel. The following derivations give alternative pronunciations of *quarter of* for (ii) and (iii).

(ii) /kwɔtr̩ ɒv/

    Stress placement ⇒ kwɔ́tr̩ əv

    /r/-realization ⇒ kwɔ́tər əv

UVD ⇒ [kwɔ́tr̩ əv]   /r/-deletion ⇒ kwɔ́tə əv

    UVD ⇒ [kwɔ́təv]

(iii) /kwɔ́tə ɒv/

    Stress placement ⇒ kwɔ́tə əv

UVD ⇒ [kwɔ́təv]   [ʔ]-insertion ⇒ [kwɔ́tə ʔəv]

(The /t/ can also be realized as [ʔ].)

PANLECTAL AND POLYLECTAL GRAMMARS

One problem to which this book is intended as a contribution is how far one system underlies all varieties of a language. This assumption (often implicit) may seem attractive at first sight in that it accounts for the notion of <u>one language</u>: all speakers of the same language have the same basic system with the variants accounted for by fairly late, realization rules, rule order differences and the like. It seems reasonable to suppose that if speakers of the same language can understand each other, then they must have the same basic system underlying their performance. However, mutual intelligibility is not a simple yes/no question. There are different degrees of intelligibility, there is intelligibility in one way only, and furthermore mutual intelligibility cuts across generally accepted language boundaries. For example, broad dialect speakers from Devon and Durham will have considerable difficulty understanding one another, whereas similarly broad speakers from Leeds and Liverpool will have far fewer problems of communication, though there may well be some. Secondly, we must note that none of these speakers have any difficulty in understanding RP as used on the radio and television, whereas speakers of RP often have difficulty in understanding broad regional accents. Thirdly, with regard to the artificiality of language

boundaries, a Low German speaker living near the
Dutch-German border has more in common linguistically
with his near Dutch neighbours than with his Bavarian
compatriots. Fourthly, it sometimes happens that two
speakers can understand each other using different
languages (cf. Dorian's study of Gaelic and English
in East Sutherland, 1982), indicating that mutual
intelligibility is certainly not a sufficient
criterion. Chomsky (1980: 117-20) concludes that the
notion of language is of little use to linguists, who,
in his view, should concentrate on grammars not
languages.

We must also take account of the speaker's knowledge of his/her own system. Our example of one-way
intelligibility demonstrates that it is possible for
a speaker of one variety to understand another without
necessarily being able to reproduce it. Let us give
a more specific example to clarify the point.
Northern English (i.e. not Scottish) speakers do not
differentiate between [ʊ] and [ʌ] in their own
systems, whereas Southern speakers, and RP speakers,
do, as in *put* and *putt* respectively. Nevertheless,
Northerners can understand radio and television news
bulletins spoken with an RP accent, and Southerners
can understand not-too-broad Northerners with respect
to this distinction. But, if we observe Northerners
and Southerners trying to mimic their counterparts
(for whatever reason), we soon see that there are two
separate vowel systems. A number of Northern speakers
(who were not brought up to do so) try to use the
[ʊ]/[ʌ] distinction: they use an unrounded vowel,
somewhere in the region of [æ̈] or [ə̈], for both
sounds. (See below for further discussion of this
from a social point of view.) Thus we hear not only
[kæ̈m] *come* and [sæ̈n] *son, sun*, but also [pæ̈t] *put* and
[bæ̈tʃə] *butcher*. These speakers simply do not know,
in the technical, linguistic sense, the difference
between these two sounds. Similarly, Southern-born
actors portraying Northerners often forget to use
[ʊ] for both sounds, using the occasional [ʌ] in
accordance with their own system: they, for their
part, do not know the lack of difference.

Misunderstandings between speakers of different
regional varieties of a language are a useful source
of evidence for linguists; many examples of this kind
of occurrence are very enlightening from the point of
view of underlying systems. If we are attempting to
establish a theory of language which claims to explain
how native speakers understand each other, we must
also investigate how it is they often misunderstand
each other as well, because even in perfect conditions

of communication misunderstandings occur. For
instance, in a seminar about the language of comedy
shows I mentioned the expression [t'ɹɒbɫ ə? ?mɪɫ]
(*trouble at the mill*). A student from the London
area wrote this down subsequently in an essay as
trouble up mill. In terms of her phonological system
[ə?] followed by a bilabial closure could only be
interpreted as *up*. Furthermore, because she was un-
used to the use of a glottal stop for the definite
article, she was unable to detect the longer hold
period of the glottal stop (during which the lips are
brought together) in comparison with the hold period
where no definite article occurs, as in *trouble at
Manchester*. In a detailed transcription of the two
utterances this difference can be indicated as
follows:

[ə? p̚m] as in *at the mill*,

[ə?m] as in *at Manchester*.

(It should be pointed out that the use of two joined
letter symbols in the first transcription gives in
this visual form an impression of greater length
than is, in fact, involved, but this is one of the
problems of letter transcriptions.)

Trudgill (1983a) presents the results of two
tests designed to ascertain the degree of predicta-
bility of syntactic forms and semantic interpretations
from various English dialects. These show that, for
the most part, linguistically sophisticated native
speakers, even those with considerable training and
experience in linguistics, fare little better than
foreigners in predicting possible sentences of some
varieties of English. On the basis of this kind of
evidence it is difficult to see how a panlectal
grammar is justifiable, and whether even a polylectal
approach is appropriate.

It is worth noting how children deal with variant
forms. If there are variant forms within the child's
immediate circle of adult models, it will tend to
waver in its usage and this may well persist in adult
speech; for instance, P's use of both [boˑk] and
[bok] for *book*, Lodge, 1983, and Y's use of both
[lɪʊk] and [lok] for *look* in Chapter 1 below, because
both had in their immediate family speakers who used
the diphthongal variant and also those who used the
monophthongal variant in such words. If a child is
exposed to regional variants only sporadically, up to
about the age of 3 or 4, it often handles them phonetically, that is to say, it imitates them; thus, a
child of Southern parents, exposed to a Northern

neighbour's [a] in *bath*, will sometimes mimic the
[a]-pronunciation. When it is older, however, the
child will tend to handle the Northern pronunciations
phonologically, that is, it will reinterpret them in
terms of its own system and will no longer attempt to
mimic them. (This is based on personal observation
during 12 years' residence in Norfolk, and it needs
much more careful and rigorous investigation.) At
some stage during the acquisition process a child
learns the equivalences between those alien accents
to which it is exposed and its own system. This
would suggest that all speakers, whatever their phonological system, learn a set of equivalences for the
English "language", but only those to which they are
exposed.

If we follow Trudgill (1983a: 29-30), we need to
separate the native speaker competence from the
speaker's ability to understand varieties other than
his/her own. In other words competence is restricted
to the native speaker's knowledge of the forms he/she
produces normally. Of course, many such grammars
overlap and this explains a speaker's ability to
understand other, not-too-dissimilar varieties.
Where varieties differ, a speaker will use a number
of different techniques, both linguistic and prag-
matic, to attempt a suitable interpretation of what
he/she has heard. If a speaker is in regular contact
with a different variety, then one technique of
comprehension would be a set of equivalence rules.
These are not performance rules, but recognition
techniques. They would be of the sort Trudgill
discusses (1974: 140-44) for relating the different
subsystems in Norwich, e.g.

$$\left. \begin{array}{c} //\bar{a}// \\ //ai// \end{array} \right\} \rightarrow //ai//.$$

This is the rule used by many Norwich speakers for
collapsing the phonological difference between
lexical items such as *name* and *nail* (see further
Chapter 6, below). In the case of RP/Stockport,
there would be a rule collapsing the *put*/*putt* distinction:

$$\left. \begin{array}{c} /\Lambda/ \\ /u/ \end{array} \right\} \rightarrow /o/(^5).$$

As an example of a rule relating Stockport and RP,
we can give the following:

$$\left.\begin{array}{l}/\varepsilon\text{\textsc{i}}/\\/\text{e:}/\end{array}\right\} \rightarrow /\text{ej}/$$

which collapses the distinction found in older Stockport speakers between *weight* with a diphthong and *wait* with a long monophthong. We must stress that equivalence rules are learnt optionally, if the (social) need for them arises, e.g. a move to a new part of the country.

A second aspect of variety comprehension that needs further investigation is the quantification of the degree of difference between dialects (cf. Trudgill, 1983a: 30). We need to establish a method of predicting mutual intelligibility, or otherwise, of different accents. Both phonological distinctions and phonetic realization are relevant to this. In a test similar to that discussed by Trudgill (1983a), already mentioned above, which I administered to a number of language and linguistics undergraduates from various parts of the United Kingdom at the University of East Anglia (⁶), the pronunciation [bʌɫ] for *bull* was rejected by Southerners and RP-speakers as non-English, no doubt on the phonological grounds of lexical incidence, but by many speakers from the North of England it was perceived as "posh" or even "RP", presumably a misinterpretation of the RP vowel system on the basis of phonetic confusion (see also above in this section). Similarly, [stɪɛ:] for *straw* is likely to cause considerable difficulty of comprehension for any speaker who says [stɪɔ:] for this word because of the phonetic distance of the two vowel phases and also because of the phonetic similarity of the former to the more common pronunciations of *stray*.

As a starting-point, then, I shall not assume the same basic underlying pan-English system for all the varieties I shall investigate. The present book is intended as a contribution to determine what all English accents do have in common and what distinguishes them one from another. There is sufficient evidence to conclude that, rather than assume an idealized speaker/hearer who has a system which is represented by formal standard spoken English, it is important to use colloquial data on which to test hypotheses (cf. Lodge, 1976 and 1970; J. Milroy, 1982: 46-47). I shall not attempt to give an exhaustive account of the phonological system of each locality; rather I have selected those distinctions and processes that are necessary for the comparison of areal and social differences.

HISTORICAL BACKGROUND

Another aspect of variety which has to be considered in attempting to establish a speaker's competence of his/her community is the historical background to the differentiation of local varieties, and the extent to which this can legitimately be said to form part of that competence. An extreme example of use of historical background in establishing a phonological system is furnished by Chomsky and Halle (1968), where details of the Great Vowel Shift are assumed to underlie the modern English vowel system, and, to quote a particular example, an underlying velar fricative is posited to account for the difference in the stressed vowels in *righteous* and *divinity* (ibid.: 234). If we consider change on a smaller scale, we find instances of competing and obsolescent forms, which have to be considered when establishing the phonological systems of a community. A few examples will suffice to demonstrate this aspect of accent varieties. Around Manchester there are three forms of the word *father* in respect of the stressed vowel: [fáðə], [fέeðə] (or an alternative with a monophthong, [fέ:ðə], depending on the quality of the vowel in words such as *gate* and *name*), and [fέ:ðə], the first two being considered old-fashioned by most speakers in the Stockport area. The first one, with its short vowel, is the modern reflex of the oblique forms in Middle English, e.g. genitive *fadres*, which has been regularized to the subject form as well. The second pronunciation is from the Middle English nominative, *fader*. In this case the short *a* was lengthened at a later period because it was in an open syllable, that is, *fa-der*; this then changed its quality, monophthongal or diphthongal, along with other words of this type, e.g. *name, gate*. The third pronunciation is a borrowing from the standard pronunciation, perhaps via the church. Although all three forms are known to Stockport speakers, as obsolescent forms, the first two would normally only be used facetiously (cf. Lodge, 1973: 86, footnote). On the other hand, in parts of Lancashire their status is different, all three being current in different groups of the community: the first two are used by many speakers over 50 years old and some younger ones in rural areas, the exact distribution of each being unknown to me, and the borrowed form is, in general, used by those under the age of 50. Sporadic use of the older forms by younger speakers would seem to be an indication of regional awareness, as opposed to facetiousness in the case of Stockport. Interpretation of any form by local speakers will help to determine its status in the system. In the case of the first two forms in Stockport, they are like fossils, learnt piecemeal, and can be represented as a listing in the grammar (even though they are the historically more "correct" forms). The same would apply to similar forms such as [kɔɪl] for *coal* (possibly a loan-pronunciation from Yorkshire rather than a relic), and [ɹɪi?] and [nɪi?] for *right* and *night* (cf. Lodge, 1973: 86), which are reflexes of the retention of the velar fricative referred to above in such words longer in the North of England than in the South, so that development along with words of the *fine*-type did not take place. (The /ɔω/-diphthong referred to in Lodge, 1973: 84, is even more of a rarity in Stockport; I have only ever heard it used regularly by one speaker, Y's father (see Chapter 1), in one word only: *Shaw* [ʃɔω] *Heath*, a district of Stockport.)

To make decisions on historical matters of this sort with regard to establishing the present system of a locality, we must have regard to whether such alternatives are known (in the technical sense) as regular forms, facetious forms, "odd" forms, and so on. We can even see cases of change in progress. For example, the /εɪ/-/e:/ distinction mentioned above (p.18) and discussed in Lodge (1973) is not known by a large number of speakers in the Stockport area, namely those who have a diphthong in *name, gate* and *wait* anyway, and this can apply to members of the same family: thus, of the six members of Y's and N's family (see Chapter 1; Lodge, 1966, 1978 and 1983), three, including N, used the distinction, three, including Y, did not. A similar case is furnished by Norwich speakers: older members of certain groups have a distinction between the vowels of *gate* with /ε:/ and *day* with /æɪ/, whereas the majority of young speakers do not have the distinction and do not know how to apply it. (This calls into question the exact interpretation of diasystem by Trudgill, 1974: 134-5, as a system common to all members of the speech community. Cf. also his own comments on this in Trudgill, 1983a: 11-12.)

LANGUAGE AND SOCIAL GROUPS
As a final consideration I now want to look at some of the social aspects of phonological variation. Since variant forms can occur within one locality and even in one and the same speaker's utterances, it is generally assumed that this variation has some kind of social significance of a group-membership kind, whereby a speaker indicates which group of people he/

she wishes to be associated with. This kind of variation is obviously different from the stylistic variation which is determined by application or otherwise of allegro rules, etc., though there may be some overlap. For example, the incidence of [?] in Stockport can be used as an indication of group membership (see further on this below), whereas the deletion of unstressed vowels is a feature of fast speech in all speakers in Stockport. On the other hand, the fast-speech feature of place of articulation harmony may be applied differentially by different groups, for example, teenagers use it more than speakers who are over sixty years old ([7]).

Much research in this area has concentrated on relating sets of linguistic variants to given social groups (e.g. Labov, 1980; Trudgill, 1974; Trudgill and Foxcroft, 1978). These groups are intuitive/traditional or based on some official set of categories (those of the Registrar General in Britain). However, it is becoming more and more evident that these categories are too gross to be of much practical value to the linguist and much finer distinctions are made by some researchers (e.g. Milroy and Milroy, 1978; Milroy, 1980; Cheshire, 1982). In what has come to be called correlational linguistics, sophisticated statistical techniques are employed to present the data in quantified terms([8]), relating patterns of variation sometimes to predetermined socio-economic groups, sometimes to smaller social groups.

As far as British English is concerned, it is the smaller social unit which seems to be the most fruitful area of research (cf. Milroy's comments, 1980: 13-14). Variety in many British contexts groups people together in a way which cuts across any socio-economic groups. It may well be that in other English-speaking countries the grosser class unit is sufficient to cope with discernible variation (though note McEntegart and Le Page's caveat about assuming knowledge of stratification of a foreign community, 1982: 123), but in the area where I have most experience, Stockport, terms like "middle class" and "working class" are very difficult to apply. It is important to stress that from the point of view of evaluation by other speakers, we have to deal with relative classifications. For example, many Southern British speakers classify Northerners as working class, even if their accent has only a few regional features. On the other hand, within the Stockport area there are many subtle differences, which only local speakers are aware of. For instance, to many speakers in Stockport the pronunciation [aːf] for *half*, rather than [af], in times of the clock, e.g. *half past three*, would be considered "snobbish, posh". This is a question of social status rather than of social class.

What I would like to propose is that there are a number of social groups within a geographical area, which are determined by a number of linguistic features. In other words, linguistic variation is not seen as a reflection of some *a priori* system of social classification, but rather as one of the factors which go towards dividing people up into social groups. (Cf. Cheshire's, 1982, discussion of non-standard features of Reading English.) I can exemplify this by using the distribution of the glottal stop in Stockport ([9]). This shows the following characteristics:

A: occurrence in word-final position as a variant of [t] or [k], and in glottally reinforced variants of [$\overset{?}{\mathrm{p}}$], [$\overset{?}{\mathrm{t}}$] and [$\overset{?}{\mathrm{k}}$];

B: glottally reinforced variants of [$\overset{?}{\mathrm{p}}$], [$\overset{?}{\mathrm{t}}$] and [$\overset{?}{\mathrm{k}}$], and as a variant of [t] in syllable-final position before consonants;

C: as A, plus occurrence in intervocalic position within a word, and use as the definite article;

D: as B, plus occurrence as the definite article.

These regularly occurring groups of linguistic variants equate in general with the following groups of people:

A = teenage girls;

B = women of 50 and older;

C = teenage boys;

D = men of 50 and older.

Some speakers show considerable variation in use, others are more consistent. Association with different groups in different contexts on the level of interpersonal encounters can be explained in terms of accommodation (see, for example, Giles and Powesland, 1975: esp. 154-81). When two speakers shift their accents slightly, each in the direction of the other, their accents converge; when two speakers emphasize the differences between their accents, they diverge. (For a discussion of the social reasons for this, see Giles and Powesland, ibid.) In the Stockport example, speakers will choose particular forms depending on which group they want

to be identified with. In certain cases the forms
chosen by a speaker will produce an evaluation by
other speakers. For example, at home a teenage girl
may conform to type A, but out with her peers in the
evening, she may well use forms of type C. Members
of other groups, for example her parents, will tend
to react adversely to certain forms not associated
with her "normal" group, e.g. the use of the glottal
stop as the definite article, and classify her as
"common" or a "tomboy".

In the same way we can interpret the use of
forms such as [kæm] *come* and [bætʃə] *butcher*,
mentioned above, as an attempt on the part of the
speaker to associate with a group considered by them
to be worthy of emulation - RP-speakers. On the other
hand, other groups, for example, members of a Stockport working-men's club, will not be impressed by such
pronunciations and will interpret them as low-valued.
As a mark of their solidarity in contrast to the
aspirations implicit in the RP-emulation, they will
use the local forms with /o/, which they value more
highly, and on occasion use "broader" forms such as
[nɪiʔ] rather than [näːʔ] for *night* (cf. Lodge, 1973:
86). In addition to this we may note that as people
change their social role, they operate with different
systems of evaluation depending on the circumstances;
thus a speaker who regularly emulates RP may also use
indigenous /o/-forms ([10]) regularly, when talking to
close relatives of their own sex, as a mark of solidarity.

We are, therefore, concerned with classification
into social groups by fellow-members of a community
via the linguistic forms used, as well as by the
linguist-observer. The members of a community are on
the whole not conscious of the linguistic indices that
they use to classify other speakers (though there is,
of course, a certain amount of *ad hoc* conscious
knowledge of linguistic differences); it is the
linguist's task to identify them. Although much work
has been done on individual indices, more investigation of the interrelationships of sets of indices
is necessary, if we are to progress beyond a piecemeal appreciation of their role.

Although in this book I shall not be going into
detail with regard to the indices of the various
social groupings within each locality, leaving that
for the future, I am assuming that the phonological
differences that I discuss in each chapter form at
least part of the total set of indices differentiating
British English accents, that is, some of the ways
whereby an Englishman can recognize a Scotsman, some-

one from Oldham can recognize someone from Stockport, and a chartered accountant can recognize a roadmender.

NOTES

1. In a very simple test I asked a number of unsophisticated English speakers to make a noun from *opaque*, by asking them to fill in the missing word in the second of the two following sentences, keeping the meaning the same: *Look at that glass - it's opaque. Look at the ...... of that glass.* In most cases there was no immediate response, but when a word was offered, it was invariably *opaqueness*, avoiding the Latinate alternation altogether. For a more thorough test and discussion, see Cutler (1980).

2. It is quite likely that alternations of the *school - scholar, join - junction* type, as discussed by Ladefoged (1982: 82) should be treated in terms of relational rules (cf. Tiersma, 1983: 73-76) rather than process rules, as a reflection of their fossilized nature.

3. /ʌ/ is an exception (see below), but this has nothing to do with morphological alternations.

4. The matching of the voice feature in the preceding context of CCS obviates the necessity of proposing a dependency degree of 3 for the deleted stops (cf. Lodge, 1981). The environments are treated differently by Guy (1980) and Neu (1980) and the rule is treated polylectally. The hierarchy of constraining environments is difficult to test on the material presented here, but I would not consider it valid for British English. Guy's notion of articulatory complexity of the cluster (1980: 9) deserves further investigation, but his morphological conditioning, referred to *passim*, does not seem to hold in the data recorded from my informants.

5. In Trudgill's example he uses the double slant lines to indicate units of the diasystemic phonological inventory. I am not concerned here with the notion of diasystem, so I simply use single slants.

6. For details, see Lodge (in preparation).

7. For a statistical treatment of one such phonological feature, t/d-deletion, see Guy (1980).

8. A full list of such works would be very large, but see, for example, Sankoff (1978), Trudgill (1978), Labov (1980), Romaine (1982), and the references therein. For a critique of such methods, see McEntegart and Le Page (1982).

9. For further details of Stockport speech, see Lodge (1966; female, aged 68), Lodge (1973) and (1978;

female, aged 16), as well as Chapter 1 of the present book. In addition I have drawn on my personal observations over many years.

[10]. We must note that although the terms *hypercorrection* and *hyperdialectalism* are used to describe certain forms (e.g. Trudgill, 1983a: 12), there is no justification for establishing "true" dialects from which certain accents deviate. (Cf. Petyt's comments on this, 1980: 27-28.) Thus, the accent with [ä] rather than [ɒ] is merely a realizational variant belonging to those accents without the [ʌ]/[ʊ] distinction.

GENERAL CONVENTIONS

The format of each chapter (except the final one) follows the same pattern. First, a general description of the phonetic features of the informant(s) including vowel diagrams, followed by the transcription of the recording of the informant(s). The extracts have been chosen to exemplify all the characteristic features of the speaker's accent occurring in the recording. Finally, each phonological process displayed by the informant(s) is discussed in detail.

The transcription follows the conventions of the IPA with the following exceptions: (i) stress is marked with an acute accent over the vowel of the syllable in question (in order to avoid making decisions about syllable boundaries); (ii) labiodental stops are written [π] and [ψ] for voiceless and voiced respectively; (iii) glottally reinforced sounds are written with the glottal stop symbol immediately above the other symbol: [ˀt], [ˀk]; (iv) the retroflex approximant is represented by [ɹ̣]; (v) affrication is marked with a following [']; (vi) creaky voice is shown by a subscript tilde: [a̰]; if there is no symbol above the tilde this indicates an indistinct vocoid transition. The following points should also be noted: I have marked unreleased stops with [˺] before other oral stops and before a pause; otherwise they are released slightly or into the following sounds; I have not always marked aspiration of the voiceless stops: these are sometimes described in the general remarks of the locality and only particularly noticeable aspiration is marked in the transcription; where [ʔ] is written between two homorganic stops (nasal or oral), the supraglottal closure is assumed to continue throughout the sequence, thus [nʔn] is written rather than [nˀn]. It is assumed that all unstressed vowels are centralized in comparison with their stressed counterparts. Partially nasalized long vowel phases have the tilde over the second part of the symbolization only, eg. [ʌõ], [aĩ].

The layout of the transcription indicates breath groups: | in the phonetic transcription, / in the orthography, and a new block (separated from the previous one by its orthographic version) indicates that another speaker has been speaking or that a considerable extract has been omitted. Hesitations and trailing off are indicated by dots. The orthographic version is not punctuated in any standard way; it is only a guide to the transcription. In citations in the text I have omitted irrelevant diacritics, in particular, stress marks.

Since I am not concerned in this book with the exact phonological interpretation of the vowel systems of the different localities, I shall simply use the most common phonetic form to represent them, as appropriate (see especially Chapter 7). In each locality I have given vowel diagrams for the most commonly occurring articulations of each informant. Where there are no instances of a known vowel, this has been noted. The dots indicating the positions of the vowels on the diagrams are a typographical convenience and represent an idealization of the variation within the vowel space. For RP vowels in examples I have used a simplified broad transcription.

I have used two abbreviations for book titles throughout:

SED = Orton, H. et al. <u>Survey of English Dialects</u>, Volumes I - IV.

SPE = Chomsky, A. N. and Halle, M. <u>The Sound Pattern of English</u>.

Map showing the localities

E = Edinburgh   S = Stockport
C = Coventry   N = Norwich
SB = Shepherd's Bush   P = Peasmarsh

Chapter One

STOCKPORT, GREATER MANCHESTER
(until 1974, in Cheshire)

The two informants from Stockport represent two
different generations of the same family. Speaker Y
is 16 years old and attends a comprehensive school
in Stockport. She is the grand-daughter of speaker
N, who is 77 years old. Although the grandfather
lived in China for two years as a very small child,
he has lived and worked in Stockport for the rest of
his life. Speaker Y has lived all her life in Stockport too; although most of her friends are likewise
local teenagers, she has several friends in Liverpool.
(Speaker N's wife is the informant for Lodge, 1966.)

(i) *General*
(For a detailed description of the phonetic characteristics of speaker Y see Lodge, 1978: 56-61.)
Closures in the oral cavity tend to be more weakly
articulated by Y than by N. This means that stops
and fricatives can be found in different utterances
of the same word, e.g. [pɛpəz] and [pɛɸəz] for
Pepper's. It also means that many of the stop
releases are slow giving an affricated sound, e.g.
[lɛtˢə] and [lɛᵗsə] for *letter*. Note that this
explains the creaky voice following occurrences of
the glottal stop, e.g. [gɑʔə̰] *got a*. Speaker N, on
the other hand, does not have this feature. The
normal lip position for both speakers is neutral.
Such rounding as does occur is effected by parting
the lips in the centre only so that the sides are
kept together. The one exception is [ø:], where the
lips protrude slightly. There is in speaker Y a
predisposition to use labio-dental articulations.
This is particularly noticeable with her r-sound:[ʋ].
A labio-dental closure is also often used as the
position of rest, e.g. [doɱ] *done* at the end of a
whole utterance. It must be stressed that this tendency to use labio-dental articulations is not caused

by a protrusion of the top teeth or some similar physical characteristic. It is a widespread feature of speakers from various parts of Lancashire and Cheshire, particularly common amongst teenagers and younger children.

(ii) *Vowel diagrams*

Speaker Y:

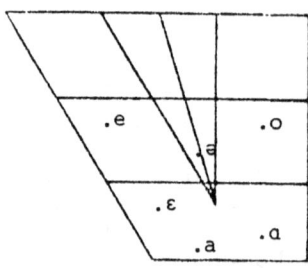

short monophthongs

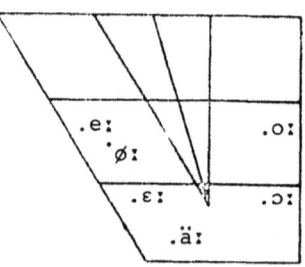

long monophthongs

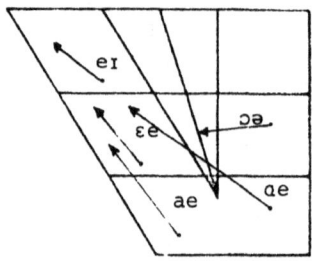

front closing
diphthongs
and [ɔə]

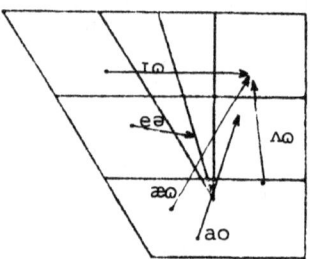

back closing
diphthongs
and [eə]

Speaker N:

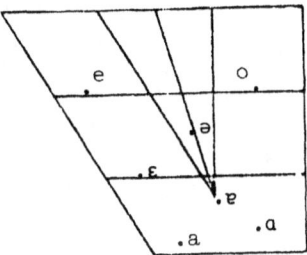

short monophthongs

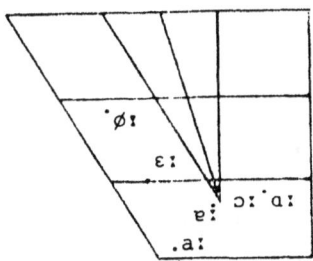

long monophthongs

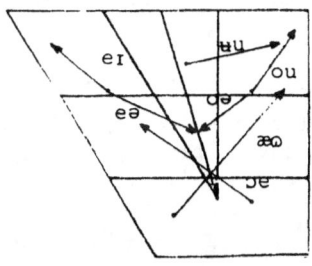

diphthongs

(There are no examples of [εe] in the extract.)

Neutral lip positions are indicated by using the IPA symbol for unrounded vowels; [e: ɛ: a:] are produced with lips spread rather than neutral by speaker Y. Note that [ɐ:] and [a:] are produced with the same tongue height and retraction but are differentiated by the lip position, neutral versus spread respectively.

(iii) *The transcription of speaker Y*

1 ɐ gá? guéeψ υán en éŋgleʃ lé? so m t'ɛ́eken ɛ́e lɛvɫ néçʃ ɟéə

   I got grade one in English Lit., so I'm taking A-level next year.

2 sɛɸ̃ ?ã́? wɑn

   Except that one.

3 aé ɛ́et' e?

   I hate it.

4 ɐ υéəɫe υáz gʎωeŋ t'¹⁰

   I really was going to ...

5 ɐ wɛ́ŋ? fəʋ ént'əvjíωz bo? ðe séz ɐ wɒŋ? gód enof | so ɐ
6 θɑ·? υáe? je k'ən sté? je dʒáβ ðɛ̃

   I went for interviews but they says I wasn't good enough / so I thought right, you can stick your job then.

7 ɐ wɛ́ŋ? fə | kədɛ́? kɑ́:s kɑs ɐ wón? ʎωɫd enof t'ə gʎω t'ə
8 nǿ:sen | bo? ʃe séz ɐ ɛŋ? gɑ́? enof ʎω lɛvɫz ɐ wón? díωen
9 enof so ʃe woɦ? geβ me n· ɐplek'ɛ́eʃɧ fám

   I went for / cadet course 'cos I wasn't old enough to go to nursing / but she says I ain't got enough O-levels I wasn't doing enough so she wouldn't give me an application form.

10 ɐ gɑ́? ə dʒáb en ə sĩωpmmɛ́:ke? ɛ̃ stɑ?pɔə? ?s dʒost ʎωpmd |
11 je ɛndʒɑ́e jesɛ́ɫ

   I got a job in a supermarket in Stockport that's just opened / You enjoy yourself.

12 no nɑ? ɑ́:ɫ lə t'ɑ́:m ðɛ t'ɛek e? en t'ǿ:z lae? je nʎω t'ə
13 υeléɪʋ péɪɸo wɛn nɛe gʎω f· ðɛ: bʋɛ́ek ɧ stóf lae? ðã? | e?s

14 ɑː υǽeʔ je ǽv ə lǽf we ðəm ɑ́ː jə noˑ
    No, not all the time they take it in turns like you know
    to relieve people when they go for their break and stuff
    like that. / It's all right, you have a laugh with them
    all you know.

15 θɹéɪ pέːz en ðə bén | ð dósbemmén ɐd ə pέːɹ éɪtʃ ən éɪ
16 néʔt ə pέː
    Three pairs in the bin / The dustbinmen had a pair each
    and he nicked a pair.

17 ɑ́ˑᵊ doũʔ υέkʧ soˑ
    I don't reckon so.

18 ef ðe sέe jɐυ tʼέm meneʔ tʼeɪ buέek ɐv έːf ən ɑ́oə
    If they say you have a ten-minute tea break, I have half
    an hour.

19 ʎωvətʼɑ́ːm ən stóf laeʔ ʔɑ́ʔ so ɐ góvə n ə sónde sómtʼɑ́ːmz
    Overtime and stuff like that, so I go over on a Sunday
    sometimes.

20 ðe gέʔ sέvntʼe fǽeβ péns ən ǽoə | sέvn̩ páoɱψ féfte
    They get 75 pence an hour / seven pound fifty.

21 ðe dóĩʔ steε ʎωpn ðe dʒos stɑ́k oɸ ʃέɫvz
    They don't stay open they just stock up shelves.

22 ɐ gɑ́ʔ tʼʎωɫd ɑf tʼʎωɫd ɐg gέʔ ðə sɑ́k kɑs ɐg gɑ́ʔ ʔtέɫ dʒɑ́md
    I got told off told I'd get the sack 'cos I'd got the till
    jammed.

23 eʔs dʒós υaeʔ ɑ́pəzepʼ buéteʃ ʎωm stóəz
    It's just right opposite British Home Stores.

24 jέː eʔs zə kɫɑ́seks nǽω ᵏgɑtʼ tʼíω bég sénəməz zέː | eʔs
25 ɫɑ́ːk je υɑ́ːʔ op ðέː ə̃j jə líωkeũ υɑ́ːʔ dǽon ɐtʼ eʔ
    Yeah it's the Classics now, it's got two big cinemas there.
    / It's like you're right up there and you're looking right
    down at it.

26 e? kaʃːᵉ tʃwénːᵈe faːβ péns aṇ ṇə βós

It costs you twenty-five pence on the bus.

27 féfteɪm péns | téʋəψö ént e? | ?e?s ɔ́ːfɫ áː gɛ? əwɛ we fɔ́ː
28 ðʌɷ | pʋesénd aṇ óndə se?stéɪn | sʌɷ ɐkʧ gɛ́? əwée weð e?
29 je nə | je gɛ́? soṇ ʋáe? déːt'e ɫɔ́?s af ðə kəndóktəz zʌ́ɷ |
30 ðɛɾ áːɫ | déd jóṇ

Fifteen pence / Terrible, isn't it? / It's awful I get away
with four though / Pretend I'm under sixteen / so I can get
away with it you know / You get some right dirty looks off
the conductors though. / They're all / dead young.

31 ?tʃɛ́endʒ ữɐ maˑeṇd | máend³ jɪɷ we máe ɛː ðɛḍ tʃɔ́? me ǽɷ? |
32 ef je gɛ́? je ɛ́ː ko? laɛ? ðá? β̃ ná? komen éə

I changed my mind / Mind you with my hair they'd chuck me
out / If you get your hair cut like that I'm not coming
here.

33 ɐ lóv aven ə móg ə tʃéken sɪɷp befáʋ ɐ ɣó t'ə bɛd wɛn ɐw̃
34 wátʃeṇ ṇə t'éle

I love having a mug of chicken soup before I go to bed when
I'm watching the telly.

35 ez ə wóg̊ ko? məʃéɪnest' | wǿːçs op áfət'ən | e ast'ə k'ɔ́?
36 áːɫ péɪsez ə wód je nʌ̇ɷ ɣaek' ə̃ méek θéṇz

He's a wood-cut machinist / works up Offerton / He has to
cut all pieces of wood you know like and make things.

37 e ɛ́e?s e? e láˑe??ᵗ ðə wán e áɗb befáːʋ e wz n əpʌ̇ɫstʋə

He hates it, he liked the one he had before, he was an
upholsterer.

38 e séḍ ðə fɛ́ɫə ðɛ́ː t'ʌ̇ɷɫm me t'ə gʌ̇ɷ daonstɛ́ːz wev som st'óφ
39 wɛ́e?ʧ fə | t'ə be dóṇ e sɛz ɐ θáːt' e? b̥ be sóm sɛt'éɪz
40 waṇπ ʋeɪk'óʋʋen ə sómθen

He said the fellow there told me to go downstairs we've
some stuff waiting for / to be done he says I thought it'd
be some settees want recovering or something.

41 job̊ bɛ́?ə léɪv ðáˑ? ʧ gɛ? nóðə wán

You'd better leave that and get another one.

42 me mée? wénde ʃeɪj beŋ góen áœ? weð ə láð fə ... | á·β beŋ
43 góen áœ? we ew̃ t'ɪ̃ɷ n ė:f jéəz ɑn sát'əde so we á went̚ t'ə
44 blá?pɪɷɫ se sɛ́ɫəbɾɛe? | wáɫ lɐd wəz sék'án e? ə̃ fel tə̃ʊ̃ψ
45 ʋáond tə ez gɪ́ɣ fʋénd e sɛz ez e á:ʋ ʋá:?

My mate Wendy she's been going out with a lad for ... /
I've been going out with him two and a half years on Saturday, so we all went to Blackpool to celebrate. / One lad
was sick on it and Phil turned round to his girl-friend he
says, Is he all right?

46 á: lóvd e? | ðə bég̚ dépə waw̃? wǿ:k'en no

I loved it / The Big Dipper wasn't working, though.

47 ɐ θá·? weᵊz góen t'ə go áf ə? ðə k'á:nə kəz e? dʒǿ:?t' ən
48 e? séɪm t'ə t'ép óp

I thought we was going to go off at the corner 'cos it
jerked and it seemed to tip up.

49 we wɛ̃ə? an n̥a? n e? ʋát'ɫz ɑ: ɫə t'á:m | ʃée?ʃe báœ?

We went on that and it rattles all the time / shakes you
about.

50 ðɛ mée? je

They make you.

51 ʃe má:? ə gɑt' én jɛ? | ? depénnz ef ʃez pást əʋ éŋɫəʃ |
52 ef ʃe dóʒ ʃe be éebə t'ə béɪ | ə | nǿ:s

She might have got in yet / It depends if she's passed her
English. / If she does, she'll be able to be / a / nurse.

53 sómθel lae? ðá? | ʃe dom? báðə

Something like that / She doesn't bother.

54 ɐ wɑ? ə dá·g̊ | ðjos t'ɐv lʌ̃ɷdz

I want a dog / They used to have loads.

55 ɐ k'ó? ðes pé?tʃʋ áœ? ?ə péepə n̥ n̥és gɪ́əɫ ʃe ad lóvle hɛ́: |
56 t'óx e? t'ə ðe ɛ́:dʋɛsə op ðə ʋʌ̃ɷd

I cut this picture out of the paper and this girl she had
lovely hair / Took it to the hairdresser up the road.

57 ɐ kʼɛ́π ɱe ɛ́ψ̊ kɔ́vəd ɔ́π fəʊ ɛ́edʒez | laɐk ə nɔ́ʔtʼə
I kept my head covered up for ages / Like a nutter.

58 jɪω ɫok áːfɫ so ɐ kʼɔ́tʼ eʔ tʼə mɛ́ek eʔ líω bɛ́tʼə kʼoz eʔ
59 ɫɔ́ʔs ə mɛ́s wae eʔ wəz̥ gʊʌωen áoʔ so e sɛz jíω ɫíωʔ tʼɛ́ɹəbɫ
60 | stʃɛ́ːpeb mán
You look awful so I cut it to make it look better because
it looked a mess while it was growing out so he says you
look terrible / Stupid man!

61 ʔʃáoʔs | e wʌω̃ʔ éʔ me e wʌω̃ʔ ǿːʔ ɛ́nebade em
He shouts / He won't hit me he won't hurt anybody him.

62 jeð θɛ́ŋk o ɛ́ɪz̥ | dɛʊ ʊɔ́f boʔ eɪ ɛ́znʔ ez zə mʌωs wɛ́ɪkes lɛ́kɫ
63 θɛ́ŋg̊
You'd think, oh he's / dead rough but he isn't he's the
most weakest little thing.

(iv) *The transcription of speaker N*

64 dáωn tʔ sɛ́llə | n ənoðə wan em peɪtəz béd'ɹoum | ðáʔ wũ we
65 ád ətʔ bɔ́kstən ɹɔ́ːd | ðáʔ wan op em péɪtəz bédɹoum wǿːk
66 ɔːɹáeʔ| eɪ fédɫz əbǽoʔ | tʼɛ́ːks θɛ́ːɹeəɫ | jə sɛ́ɪ ɐ wǿːk oɸ
67 ən ɛ́ndoəɹ ɛ́ːɹeəɫ ən eʔs vɛ́ɹe kɹɛ́tecl wɛ́ː jə gɛ́ʔ ðe ɛ́ːɹeəɫ |
68 gɛt et en ə pɹápə spáʔ fɔɹ em tə gɛ́t ə gɔdʔ péktʃə naʔ | goz
69 m pɔ́ɫz eʔ dǽωn əm pɔ́ʔs eʔ sɔ́mwɛːɹ ɛ́ɫs | e kʼáːŋʔ gɛɹ ə gɔ́bʔ
70 péktʃə
Down the cellar / and another one in Peter's bedroom / That
one we had at Buxton Road / That one up in Peter's bedroom
works alright / He fiddles about / takes the aerial / You
see I work up an indoor aerial and it's very critical where
you get the aerial / get it in a proper spot for him to get
a good picture and that / Goes and pulls it down and puts
it somewhere else / He can't get a good picture.

71 nɛ́ks dóə bəʔ wán ʃez̥ pɔ́ʔ θɹɛ́ɪ pɛ́ːɹ əv pɔ́ːɫəɹoedʔ ɹlásez en
72 nə bɛ́n ən ə pɛ́ːɹ ə njúu ʃúuz bjúuteɫ pɛ́ːɹ ə ʃúuz | ən ə

73 pέːɹ ə njʉ́u sláˀks | en ˀ dósben
   Next door but one she's put three pair of polaroid glasses
   in the bin and a pair of new shoes, beautiful pair of
   shoes / and a pair of new slacks / in the dustbin.

74 ᵊdóːnˀ θéŋk ɐv έvə bóːt ɛne
   I don't think I've ever bought any.

75 wɫ láˀ pέːɹ opstέːz ɐ fǽɷn ném an | sǽɷθse bέɪtʃ | pέːɹ ə
76 wáː ˀɹémd wónz ze áː jə noː | ɐ gát ə pέːɹ ə ðém əz góz
77 ensáːd jə óːnnɹe glaseẓ | áː spέʃɫess séː | jə ʃónṇˀ wέːɹ
78 əm
   Well that pair upstairs I found them on / Southsea beach /
   Pair of white-rimmed ones they are you know / I got a pair
   of them as goes inside your ordinary glasses / Eye specialists say / you shouldn't wear them.

79 wǿːks ɑf ˀ káː bát'ɹe | ɑɹ etɫ̣ wǿːk ɑf ˀ méːnz | eɪ móks
80 əbǽɷˀ we ðáˀ
   Works off the car battery / or it'll work off the mains /
   He mucks about with that.

81 eɪ dóz ez óːlez móken əbǽɷˀ bénden ˀθέːɹeəɫ
   He does, he's always mucking about bending the aerial.

82 jə nóː wət ə wəz lésnen tʉ́u óːɫ θɹʉ́u | tʃəkáfskez féfθ
   You know what I was listening to all through? /
   Tchaikovsky's Fifth.

83 ɐ wəz zέːɹ ɑm me óːŋ kwáː láːk | ˀsnáˀ bäd mjʉ́uzek̚
   I was there on my own quiet like / It's not bad music.

84 az e ʃóːn jə ˀ benákəɫəz e gáˀ æɷt ə téskoː
   Has he shown you the binoculars he got out of Tesco?

85 nɑˀ spóːs ˀ beɪ
   Not supposed to be.

86 ä dóːnˀ no wáˀ jə bóːˀ ðém θéŋ fɑ ðɛ nóː gód̚

37

I don't know what you bought them things for, they're no good.

87 ə tʃéɪpʾ péːɹ ə benɑ́kjətəz

A cheap pair of binoculars.

88 sótʃ əz zá? wɑ́ntedʾ páenten æɒtʾ tə ðá? blóːkʾ tʾoðə náːt o
89 əz ɑ́ːgjen əbæɒ? bɹéteʃ kɑ́ːz ən sǿːves | et éznt̚ bɹéteʃ
90 kɑ́ːz əz fɔ́ːlz dáon | sə mótʃ | fɑ́ɹen kɑ́ːz dóz etʾ

Such as that wanted pointing out to that bloke the other night, who was arguing about British cars and service / It isn't British cars as falls down / so much / foreign cars does it.

91 ə délekət əː enstʾɹókʃəm bʉ́uk ɒn ...

A delicate er instruction book on ...

92 jə gét sóː mənə stjʉ́udn̥ts ɒn fɑ́ɹen léŋgwedʒez dóː? jə | ə
93 koəs fɹénʃ öː be ðə fǿːs wɑ́n

You get so many students on foreign languages, don't you? / Of course French'll be the first one.

(v) *Phonological discussion*
Inventory and distinction characteristics of the Stockport system are negative ones in comparison to several of the other accents presented in this book. The most important features are: no /o/-/ʌ/ distinction, no /h/, no post-vocalic [r] before another consonant, no /n/-/ŋ/ distinction. [ŋ] without a following [g] occurs before another consonant as a product of CCS (cf. Lodge, 1966 and 1981, and below for further discussion; see also Knowles, 1978: 85). Informant N has a vocalic distinction which Y does not: /eː/-/εe/(^{1}), as in *wait/weight* respectively. (This is not in the recorded material, but see Lodge, 1973.) The phonetic realization of /ae/ varies somewhat for both informants. N has a long monophthong, [äː] *eye* (77), which has the retracted tongue position of some realizations of /aː/, e.g. [kʾäːŋ?] *can't* (69), or he has a diphthong [ae], as in [ɒːɹae?] *alright* (66); Y has similar realizations, e.g. [tʾaːm] *time* (12), [ʋae?] *right* (6), but the former is kept phonetically distinct from /ɐː/ in terms of lip position (see (ii) above). Short vowels other than /ə/ and /e/ occur in unstressed syllables.

/r/ is realized as [ɹ] by N, but mostly as [ʋ] by Y, though [ɹ] is used as a link sometimes and occurs after /θ/, e.g. [pɛːɹ eɪtʃ] *pair each* (15) and [θɹeɪ] *three* (15). There is one example of a flap as a link: [ðɛɾ ɑːɫ] *they're all* (30).

The distribution and occurrence of [ʔ] is of particular interest. (For some discussion, see the Introduction.) For Y it is the realization of /t/ in word-final position, before tautosyllabic obstruents and in syllable-final position before all non-syllabic consonants, e.g. [gɑʔ] *got* (8), [eʔs] *it's* (13), [eʔ lɪɵʔ] *it look* (58). Before syllabic /l/, however, we find [t]: compare [ʋatˈɫ̩z] *rattles* (40) and [wɛeʔṭ] *waiting* (39). Occasionally, Y uses intervocalic [ʔ] within a word, e.g. [bɛʔə] *better* (41). She also uses it as the realization of /k/ in word-final position, utterance-finally and before consonants, especially in *like*, e.g. (12), and before /t/ within a word, e.g. [neʔt] *nicked* (16). Glottal reinforcement is likewise widespread in her speech. (Her habits in this respect are in line with those of group A, as described in the Introduction.)

N, on the other hand, uses it only as a realization of syllable-final /t/ before consonants, whether word-final or not, and in glottal reinforcement. The major difference between the two speakers is use of [ʔ] for the definite article. Y uses it only sporadically: [ʔtel] *the till* (22) (cf. also [ʔ˞las] *the last* from Lodge, 1978: 67, line 119). However, in both instances the preceding sound is [ʔ], so that they could be interpreted as a conditioned variant of /ð/, cf. [laeʔ ʔa̰ʔ] *like that* (19), with the subsequent operation of UVD, cf. [ð dosbemmen] *the dustbinmen* (15). N, on the other hand, uses it regularly, though not exclusively, with alternant forms depending on the environment. *The* has the variant forms of most accents: [ðə] + C, [ðe] + V, with consonantal harmony applying to the initial consonant as described in Lodge (1981). The distribution of the other forms is as follows:

[t]   [ʔ]/[t̰]   [θ]

[tˈoðə] (88) [daɒn t̰ sɛllə] (64) [θ ɛːɹeəɫ] (66)

              [en ʔ dosben] (73)   [ʔθ ɛːɹeəɫ] (81)

              [af ʔ kä:] (79)

              [af ʔ meːnz] (79)

              [jə ʔ benak̰əɫəz] (84)

Thus, we have the exceptional form with [tˈ] only in *the other* (though a form [θ oðə], not recorded here,

39

is also used in Stockport, cf. SED III: 1065); before consonants we have [ʔ] with a simultaneous alveolar closure between alveolar sounds; before vowels [θ], though following continuants and vowels the form is [ʔθ]. (There are no recorded examples of the latter in the material I am using; an example would be: [fə ʔθ ɛːɹeəɫ] *for the aerial*.)

The question as to what the underlying form is is somewhat complex. If /t/ is chosen, since it is the phonological element to which most occurrences of [ʔ] are related, we have its regular realization, mostly without oral closure, in syllable-final position, the vowel of the article being deleted first by UVD. In this case we have the derivation as in (*1*).

(*1*) /ɑf tV meːnz/([2])

    Stress placement   ⇒   ɑf tə mé:nz

    UVD   ⇒   ɑf t mé:nz

    /t/-realization   ⇒   [ɑf ʔ mé:nz]

(I have left the intermediate stages of the derivation without brackets to indicate that their exact phonological status is undetermined. For some discussion of intermediate status, specifically related to SPE, see Fudge, 1967.) The prevocalic instances involve the addition of [θ] and, after obstruents, the deletion of [t]. We thus have the derivations (*2*) and (*3*).

(*2*) /teːks tV ɛːɹeəl/

    Stress placement   ⇒   té:ks tə ɛ́:ɹeəl

    UVD   ⇒   té:ks t ɛ́:ɹeəl

    θ-insertion   ⇒   té:ks tθ ɛ́:ɹeəl

    CCS   ⇒   [teːks θ ɛ́:ɹeəɫ]

(*3*) /-en tV ɛːɹeəl/

    Stress placement   ⇒   -en tə ɛ́:ɹeəl

    UDV   ⇒   -en t ɛ́:ɹeəl

    θ-insertion   ⇒   -en tθ ɛ́:ɹeəl

    /t/-realization   ⇒   [-en ʔθ ɛ́:ɹeəɫ]

CCS does not apply to /t/ after nasals (cf. Lodge, 1981: 34).

The main problem with this solution is the unmotivated θ-insertion rule; it is *ad hoc* to this particular lexical item. Furthermore, there is no obvious relationship between these forms and the forms with initial /ð/. An alternative solution would be to posit an underlying /θV/ for the article. This would indicate more clearly the relationship with /ðV/([3]), giving speakers the option of a "voiced" or a "voiceless" article, depending on certain social considerations. (The factors determining this choice are unclear to me, but include sex of the speaker, sex of the hearer(s), and their perceived social status.) The rules involved would then be:

(1')   /ɑf θV meːnz/

Stress placement ⇒ ɑf θə mé:nz

UVD ⇒ ɑf θ mé:nz

t-insertion ⇒ ɑf tθ mé:nz

CCS ⇒ ɑf t mé:nz

/t/-realization ⇒ [ɑf ʔ mé:nz]

(2')   /teːks θV ɛːɹeəl/

Stress placement ⇒ téːks θə ɛ́ːɹeəl

UVD ⇒ [téːks θ ɛ́ːɹeəɫ]

(3')   /-en θV ɛːɹeəl/

Stress placement ⇒ -en θə ɛ́ːɹeəl

UVD ⇒ -en θ ɛ́ːɹeəl

t-insertion ⇒ -en tθ ɛ́ːɹeəl

/t/-realization ⇒ [-en ʔθ ɛ́ːɹeəɫ]

This is preferable to the analysis as /tV/ because of the clearer representation of the relationship with /ðV/ and the avoidance of the *ad hoc* rule of θ-insertion. The t-insertion rule, on the other hand, represents part of a general insertion phenomenon, stop epenthesis, which has operated at various times throughout the history of English (eg. the /b/ in *thimble*, /d/ in *thunder*, etc. cf. Strang, 1970: 166, and Anderson and Jones, 1977: 130). In (1') the rule deleting θ can either be seen as an extension of CCS (which applies elsewhere, too, e.g. in words such as *fifths, sixths* and *months*), or as a simplification of an otherwise impossible syllable-initial cluster θ + obstruent.

In either solution the one remaining problem is absolute initial [ʔ] before consonants (no examples recorded), as in [ʔ bos ez komen] *The bus is coming*.

This cannot be accounted for by the rules given so far, but since the available material is insufficient to give a proper analysis, I shall leave this unanswered here, though I shall return to this problem in the last chapter([4]).

There is a constraint on the occurrence of [ʔ] for both informants: a sequence ʔV̆ʔ, where V̆ = unstressed vowel, either [ə] or [e], is ruled out, except in absolute initial sequences with an added glottal onset, as in [ʔeʔs] (27). Thus, we find [ɛ́nt̃ eʔ] *isn't it?* (27), but not *[ɛ́nʔ eʔ]([5]).

I shall now turn to the phonological processes, which are more widespread in Y's than in N's speech.

(a) *Lenition.* The most common lenition in Stockport is stop → fricative (cf. Lodge, 1981: 20-22):

[peɪɸo] *people* (13)

[n̥ə βos] *the bus* (26)

[pʋesɛnd] *pretend* (28)

[ɐ ɣo] *I go* (33)

[tox eʔ] *took it* (56)

[oɸ ən] *up an* (66-67).

The other lenition process, which occurs quite often, is the vocalization or even deletion of /l/, e.g.

[nʌω ʁaek] *know like* (36)

[gɪʁ fʋɛnd] *girl friend* (45)

[wae eʔ] *while it* (59).

There are no examples of this in N's speech.

(b) *Harmony.* Consonantal harmony is widespread in Y's speech, less so in N's (see Lodge, 1981, for a detailed discussion of this process in Stockport). It is the alveolar series, /t d n s z/, in particular, which harmonize in preconsonantal position to the place of articulation of the following consonant, e.g.

[tɛm menẽʔ] *ten-minute* (18)

[feftɛɪm pɛns] *fifteen pence* (27)

[soŋ ʋaeʔ] *some right* (29)

[ŋ̊ n̥ə] *on the* (20)

[jobʼ bɛʔə] *you'd better* (41)

[sɛd̪ ðə] *said the* (38)

[woɡʼ koʔ] *wood-cut* (35)

[o:ŋ kwä:ʔ] *own quiet* (83)

[gobˀ pektʃə] *good picture* (69-70).

Note that in N's case harmony is not so consistently applied as by Y: [godˀ pektʃə] also occurs in line (68). In the case of /t/ the realizations are found both with and without supraglottal closure:

[apəzepˀ buetɛʃ] *opposite British* (23)

[kədɛʔ kɑ:s] *cadet course* (7).

In the case of /-nd/ and /-nt/ the harmony applies to both segments, e.g.

[paoɱʋ fefte] *pound fifty* (20)

[dom̰ʔ bɑðə] *doesn't bother* (53)

[wɛɱʔ fə] *went for* (5) and (7)

[woɧʔ geβ] *wouldn't give* (9).

(In the case of /-nt/ the supraglottal closure is held throughout the glottal one.)

Syllabic /n/ often harmonizes with the preceding consonant, e.g.

[ʌɷpm̩d] *opened* (10)

[buɛek̬ ɧ̰] *break and* (13).

Palatalization of /t d s z/ occurs before /j/. /s/ is most consistently palatalized; there are exceptions for /d/ and /z/, e.g.

[ʃɛeʔʃe] *shakes you* (49)

[maend³ jɪɷ] *mind you* (31)

[dɛd joŋ] *dead young* (30)

[sɛz jɪɷ] *says you* (59).

Some examples involve CCS (see next section) as well as harmony, e.g.

[nɛçʃ jeə] *next year* (1)

[kaʃ^e_o] *costs you* (26).

Word-initial [ʃ] also produces harmony in the appropriate preceding consonant (for details, see Lodge, 1981: 27-28), e.g.

[doʒ̊ ʃe] *does she* (52).

With /t/, which is realized mostly as [ʔ] in word-final position, no harmony can take place, e.g.

[gɛʔ je] *get your* (32).

Occasionally harmony occurs within a word, e.g.

[stʃəːpeb] *stupid* (60).

N has two palatal articulations, which may be interpreted as instances of harmony, not found in Y's speech,

[kɹetecl] *critical* (67)

[poːɫəɹoed̚ ɟlasez] *polaroid glasses* (71).

He also uses a velar articulation, as in:

[ɔːnɲɹe glasez] *ordinary glasses* (77).

From these examples it is difficult to see exactly what the conditioning environment is, though it is probably the place of articulation of the preceding sound (bearing in mind that the final vowel of *ordinary* is centralized because it is unstressed, whereas the unstressed vowel in *critical* is not centralized, perhaps under the influence of the stressed [e]). We may note further that a number of speakers in the Stockport area have such articulations for /kl/ and /gl/ and that the exact point of contact on the roof of the mouth for /l/-realizations and the posture of the rest of the tongue varies quite a lot depending on the surrounding sounds (cf. Lodge, 1978: 61).

Another kind of place harmony is to be found only in Y's speech, as can be seen from the alternation of bilabial and labiodental articulations, e.g.

[geβ me] *give me* (9)

[faːβ pɛns] *five pence* (20) and (26)

[stoɸ wɛeʔt͡ɸ] *stuff waiting* (38-39)

[a·β beŋ] *I've been* (42).

In addition Y also displays a tendency to harmonize consonants to a labiodental place of articulation even when there are intervening vowels, e.g.

[gʊɛeѱ ʋan] *grade one* (1)

[tɛʋəѱo] *terrible* (27)

[ʋeəɫe ʋaz] *really was* (4).

In the last example there is also an intervening lingual consonant, but this does not affect the labiodental posture. (For a discussion of this in relation to child language, see Lodge, 1983, and cf. Stampe's comments on non-contiguous harmony, 1979: 76.) A particularly striking example of labiodental harmony is:

[ɐ kɛπ ŋe ɛψ kovəd oπ fəʊ ɛedʒez]

I kept my head covered up for ages (57).

This could be seen as a "left-over" from the acquisition period.

The dentals /θ/ and /ð/ harmonize with alveolar fricatives both before and after them (cf. Lodge, 1981: 29). There are no examples of /θ/ in the texts in this position, only of /ð/, e.g.

[eʔs zə] *it's the* (24)

[senəməz zɛː] *cinemas there* (24)

[əz zaʔ] *as that* (88).

We shall consider /ð/ further below.

The other main type of harmony, that of manner (in addition to place harmony in most cases), is only found in Y's speech, e.g.

[waw̃ʔ wø:ken] *wasn't working* (46)

[lɪɒkeʊ̃ ʋaːʔ] *looking right* (25)

[doʊ̃ʔ ʋɛk̬] *don't reckon* (17)

[wat̃ lɐd] *one lad* (44)

[ə̃j jə] *and you're* (25).

Although the sound most commonly affected is /n/, we also find manner harmony with /m l ð/ and occasionally the oral stops, too, e.g.

[an̥ n̥ə] *on the* (26)

[ɐw̃ watʃen] *I'm watching* (33-34)

[aːʊ ʋaːʔ] *all right* (45)

[aːɬ lə] *all the* (12)

[laeʔ ʔa̰ʔ] *like that* (19)

[lað fə] *lad for* (42)

[nɛçʃ] *next* (1)

[dʒaβ ðɛ̃] *job then* (6)

[dɛʊ ʋof] *dead rough* (62).

With the exception of /ð/→[ʔ] 'and [n̥], these examples of manner harmony follow the direction of lenition, that is, stops become fricatives or frictionless continuants, but not the other way round.

In one instance /d/ has harmonized as to place and nasality, giving: [tʌɶɬm me] *told me* (38).

Harmony of nasality only also occurs but is not common:

[ʌɷpn̩ ð̃e] *open they* (21)

[depɛnnz] *depends* (51).

There is also an example of vocalization of syllabic /l/:

[peɪɸo wɛn] *people when* (13),

which could also be the explanation for the vocalization of initial /l/ in *know like*, given above under lenition.

(c) *CCS*. Consonantal cluster simplification applies to both speakers. There are several examples from Stockport given in the Introduction and I shall not repeat them here. They affect /t/ and /d/ interconsonantally. Some of the examples also involve harmony, and we find both unsimplified and simplified clusters with harmony. Consider the following:

/paond fefte/

Place Harmony ⇒ [-ŋψ f-]

/seɪmd tə/

CCS ⇒ [-m tə]

/and pots/

Place Harmony ⇒ -mb p-

CCS ⇒ [-m p-].

The situation is somewhat different for /n/ before /t/: it is the /n/ that is deleted whether there are consonants following /t/ or not, e.g. [wɑʔ ə] *want a* (54). However, it is common for the nasality to remain, as in [wʌɑ̃ʔ ø:ʔ] *won't hurt* (61), [doʊ̃ʔ jə] *don't you* (92). Nasal harmony followed by /n/-deletion (cf. Hyman's discussion of French, 1975: 130-31) will only account for the forms with nasalized vowels; the non-nasal forms would require a further nasality-deletion rule, optional before /t/. On the other hand, if the rules can apply in either order, the non-nasalized forms would be accounted for by /n/-deletion alone.

In the sequence /ng/ the /n/ behaves differently in the unstressed endings /-eng/ and /-θeng/ from elsewhere, including stressed /θeng/. Thus, we find [komen] *coming* (32), [somθen] *something* (40), [θeŋg̊]

thing (63) and [θeŋz] *things* (36). In the last two
examples the nasal is velar, i.e. it has harmonized
with the following /g/, deleted by CCS in *things*.
In the first two examples, though, we have an alveolar nasal. Furthermore, this unstressed *-ing* ending
shows the place harmonies displayed by /n/, e.g.

    [wɑtʃen̪ n̪ə] (34)

    [wɛeʔt̪ fə] (39)

    [somθeĩ laeʔ] (53).

We thus need to distinguish the *-(th)ing* endings from
the other occurrences of /-ng/. In the latter case
the /n/ is subject to velar harmony, then CCS applies
to delete the /g/, when there is a following consonant,
e.g.

                    /θengz/

    Place Harmony   ⇒   θeŋgz

    CCS   ⇒   [θeŋz] (36).

In absolute final position, where CCS does not apply,
the /g/ sometimes is deleted, but not always; thus,
[θeŋg̊] (63), but [joŋ] (30). There is also fluctuation within a word; compare [eŋɬəʃ] (51) with
[eŋgleʃ] (1). This example seems to indicate a
fluctuation in syllable structure; CCS only applies
to a stop articulation in the coda of a syllable, so
the former example must have the boundary after the
/g/, whereas the latter one has it before the /g/.

    With the unstressed endings there are two possi-
bilities. They may behave exactly like stressed
/-eng/, e.g.

                    /-eng t-/

    Place Harmony   ⇒   -eŋg t-

    CCS   ⇒   [-eŋ t-] (4).

Otherwise /g/ is deleted before any harmony takes
place, e.g.

                    /-eng l-/

    /g/-deletion   ⇒   -en l-

    Manner Harmony ⇒   [-eĩ l-] (53).

This is not CCS, because the same deletion takes
place before a vowel, e.g. [goen ɑœʔ] *going out* (42)
([6]).

    Finally, we may note that there are more complex
derivations, as follows:

/-eng ʋ-/

/g/-deletion ⇒ -en ʋ-

Place Harmony ⇒ -eŋ ʋ-

Manner Harmony ⇒ [-eʊ̃ ʋ-] (25)

/-εkst j-/

CCS ⇒ -εks j-

Place Harmony ⇒ -εkʃ j-

Manner Harmony ⇒ [-εçʃ j-] (1).

There are two late, optional rules, which can apply after CCS and Harmony, as exemplified by the following instance:

/-sts j-/

CCS ⇒ -ss j-

Place Harmony ⇒ -ʃʃ j-

Geminate Simplif. ⇒ -ʃ j-

/j/-deletion ⇒ [-ʃe̥] (26).

Palatal harmony applies to all identical preceding alveolars (cf. Lodge, 1981: 37). Geminate Simplification and /j/-deletion are characteristic of rapid speech. The former applies to all such sound sequences, e.g. [ɑː ɨə] *all the* (49), though it is optional as demonstrated by [spεʃɨess seː] *specialists say* (77). The latter rule applies after [ʃ] and [ʒ] across a word- or syllable-boundary, when the word with initial /j/ is unstressed, cf. also [ʃεeˀʃe] *shakes you* (49).

(d) *UVD*. The circumstances under which this rule applies are difficult to determine in any general way. It is optional and not applied regularly. The commonest occurrence is loss of initial unstressed vowels, especially in absolute initial position or after vowels, e.g.

[so m] *so I'm* (1)

[sεɸ̂ˀ] *except* (2)

[govə] *go over* (19)

[ˀtʃεendʒ] *I changed* (31)

[ʃεeˀʃe baœˀ] *shakes you about* (49)

[ˀdepεnnz] *it depends* (51)

[ʔʃaoʔs] *He shouts* (61)

[goz] *He goes* (68)

[ʔs] *It's* (83).

A preceding glottal stop also appears to bring about the loss of an unstressed vowel, e.g.

[stɑʔpɔəʔ ʔs] *Stockport that's* (10)

[eʔ~b] *it would* (39)

[aeʔ ʔə] *out of the* (55)

[spoːs ʔ beɪ] *supposed to be* (85).

See also above for the treatment of the glottal stop as the definite article, where UVD is involved.

The unstressed auxiliary verbs, *an*, *and* and *not* in particular can lose their syllabicity when the surrounding sounds are vowels or semi-vowels (/j/ and /w/), e.g. [ewznep-] (37), with two syllables rather than four, and [wɒnʔ] *wasn't* (8) alongside [wɒnʔ] (7).

The other main instances of UVD are those discussed in the Introduction, where CV́CəCə is reduced to CV́CCə, where C = at least one consonant, and the final vowel may also be [e], e.g.

[əpʌɷɫstʊə] *upholsterer* (37)

[batˈɹe] *battery* (79).

(e) *Linking r*. Both informants use linking r extensively, but not on every occasion where it might apply, e.g.

[ðɛː ə̃j] *there and* (25)

[jə ɔːnnɹe] *your ordinary* (77).

Y uses [ʊ], [ɪ] and [ɾ] as links, the former being the most common. The link only occurs after [ə], [ɐː] (or [äː]), [øː] and [ɔː] (or [ɑː])([7]).

NOTES

[1]. For one possible interpretation of the Stockport diphthongs, see Lodge (1973).

[2]. The precise nature of the underlying vowel phase of the article is not important here; V represents some kind of full vowel.

[3]. On the history of the definite article, see, for example, Strang (1970). The historical relationship would also be captured in this analysis. The [θ]~[ð] (Strang, ibid.: 181) alternations could perhaps also be incorporated by means of realization rules operating on one underlying dental fricative

(cf. Fudge, 1969b: 271), but I shall not pursue this further here.

⁴. For a considerable amount of raw data, presented without any analysis, the reader is referred to the SED. In Stockport, before vowels [θ] is used in absolute initial position; before most consonants [ʔ] is used, though in the case of frictionless continuants, both can occur.

⁵. It is worth noting that this is a right-to-left constraint and is evidence for "advance planning" of articulatory moves in speech (cf. Hardcastle, 1981 and refs.). There is a similar constraint in Norwich (Trudgill, 1974: 174-75).

⁶. The /g/-deletion is *ad hoc* to these forms only, unlike in some of the other accents presented in this book. Historically the participle ending in /n/ has a different origin from that ending in /ng/ (cf. Strang, 1970: 238). It would be possible, therefore, to have two alternative participial forms, one with /-n/, the other with /-ng/, avoiding the need for a separate /g/-deletion rule. The unstressed *-thing* ending would also have to be given these alternative forms, even though they are historically not justified in this case. This could be seen as an analogical spread from the participles.

⁷. It is possible that there are circumstances where a link would never be used, but there is no evidence of this in the extracts. In *Shaw Heath*, for example, I have never heard a link used. This may be explained by the fact that in older forms of Stockport speech the first word would have had a back closing diphthong (cf. the Introduction, above), which would not allow a link anyway.

Chapter Two

SHEPHERD'S BUSH, LONDON, W12

There is one informant, C, aged 60. She was born in Shepherd's Bush, moved to Northolt in 1938, and to Norfolk in 1970. There has been no noticeable adoption of any Norfolk pronunciations. A comparison with Cockney pronunciation shows up a number of differences (see, for example, Wells, 1982: 301-34).

(i) *General*
Most stops have a complete closure, though there is a tendency to produce flaps in intervocalic position. In the release phase only [t] is ever affricated. A slight amount of creaky voice is sometimes to be heard in the vicinity of a glottal stop. The lips are rounded by slight protrusion of the lips with a corresponding drawing in at the sides. Non-rounded lip positions are either spread or neutral, depending on the stress of the syllable in question.

(ii) *Vowel diagrams*

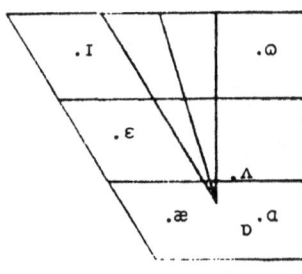 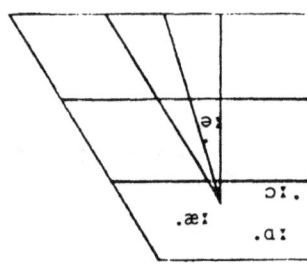

short stressed   long stressed

51

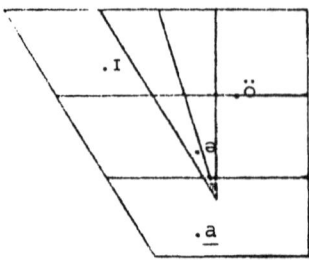

unstressed

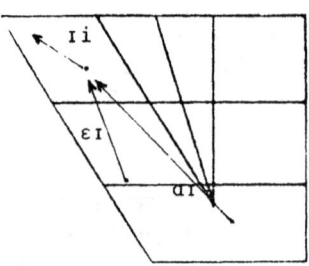

front closing diphthongs
(No examples of [ɔɪ].)

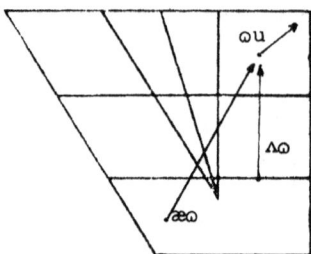

back closing diphthongs

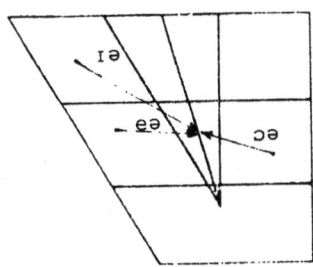

centring diphthongs

Unstressed vowels have neutral lip position, except for [ö] and [ɷ] which have no lip protrusion but drawn-in sides.

(iii) *The transcription*

1 aɪ ɔ́:wɪʒ jǿus t'æv máɪn ᴵʔjǿus tə fɔ́:ö ðǽʔ wɛ́ɪ | ðǽʔs ɔ́:ö
2 kʌ́mɪŋ bǽk næɷ ʃʌ́ɷdə lɛ́ŋθ heə ən ɪʔ sɛ́d jə nʌ́ɷ nɪ́id' tə hǽv |
3 a θɪŋk av stɪ́ö gá? ðə p'ɛ́ɪpəɪ a wəz gʌ́ɷnə bɹɪ́ŋ ɪʔ ɹáɷn:
4 bət aɪ dʒʌs kǿdn? pǿ? ma hǽ:nd ɒn ɪʔ | ɪʔs mɔ́:ɹ ə lɛ́s ðə
5 stáɪö wɒʔ ðɛɪ jǿus t'æv | dʒʌs ðɪ ɛ́:nd' tɛ́:nd ʌ́p ə bɪt'

I always used to have mine – it used to fall that way / that's all coming back now shoulder-length hair and it said you no need to have / I think I've still got the paper I was going to bring it round but I just couldn't put my hand on it / it's more or less the style what they used to have / Just the end turned up a bit.

6 wɛl a dʌ́ɷ̃? θɪ̃? máɪz vɛɹɪi má:vɫəs ɪz ɪʔ ɹɪ́iᵊɫɪi aɪ dənʌ́ɷ

Well, I don't think mine's very marvellous is it really? I don't know.

7 wɛɫ lɪ ʌ́ðə wɪ́ik aɪ dʒʌs kǿdnt' dou ə θɪ́ŋ wɪ̊ð ɪd ɪʔ sɪɪnd
8 ʔǽbsəlóuʔtlɪi hʌ́ɷplɪs | bəʔ sætədɛɪ ɪʔ sɪ́im tə dʒəs gʌ́ɷ
9 ʔɪ́izəɫɪ əʒ jou wɒ́ntəd e̥t

Well, the other week I just couldn't do a thing with it, it

53

seemed absolutely hopeless / but Saturday it seemed to just go easily as you wanted it.

10 jə gɛ́? sʌm ínɛkspɹíiᵊɹɪənssɪt wʌ́nz a səp'ʌ́ωz
You get some inexperienced ones I suppose.

11 a θíⁱ? ðeɪ dʒʌ́s gʌ́ω tω ə ʃɒ́p' dʌ́ω̃? ðɛɪ | ðǽ?s wɒt aɪ θíŋk
12 əbaωp maɪ sʌ́nz wáɪf | bɪkʊ ʃɪz gʊ? nʌ́ω sətífɪkɪts əɹ
13 ɛ́nɪθɪŋ? fə hɛ́ədɹɛsɪŋ əɹ ɛ́nɪθɪŋ aṹ ʃɔ́:ᵊ ðæ?s wɒ? ʃíi mʌ́st
14 əv dʌ́n

I think they just go to a shop, don't they? / That's what I think about my son's wife / because she's got no certificates or anything for hairdressing or anything I'm sure that's what she must have done.

15 nʌ́:ω a səpʌ́ω | ðɛ θíŋk ʌωɛl ɪ?s ə pɛ́:m ən ɪ?s táɪdɪ ən nǽ?s
16 ít

No, I suppose / they think, oh well it's a perm and it's tidy and that's it.

17 bʌt ðɛ wɒ́z əm ə tɔ́:k sʌm wáɪł əgʌ́ω əbáωt ðíiz píipł hǽvɪŋ
18 t'ou gʌ́ω | jə nʌ́ω ł lɹiz hɛ́ədɹɛsɪŋ píipł st'á:tɪŋ ʌ́p ? hʌ́ωm
19 ən ɔ́:ł lís bíznɪs

But there was m a talk some while ago about these people having to go / you know all these hairdressing people starting up at home and all this business.

20 kɒz jʊv gʊ́? nʌ́ω kléɪm ɒŋ ŋəm ǽv jou ʊɹ ɛ́nɪθɪŋ ɪf sʌ́mθɪŋ
21 hǽpmn̩d ɪf ðeɪ géɪv jou ə pɛ́:m ən ɪ? ɹóuɪndʒə héə wɛ wɒ́?
22 kʊdʒω dóu | jɔ wʌ́n ǽv ə lég' tə stǽ:nd ɒn wɒ́dʒö ɹíːəłɪ |
23 ðǽ:?s sə tɹʌ́bö

Cos you've got no claim on them, have you, or anything if something happened if they gave you a perm and it ruined your hair, well what could you do? / You wouldn't have a leg to stand on, would you, really? / That's the trouble.

24 sʌ́m píipł ðeɪ wö wɒ́n? nís dʌ́n | ɹíilɪ ɪ?s sɛɹ ʌ́ωɪ ɹísk ën
25 e? ɪf ðɛɪ ǽv vɹiz θɪŋz dʌ́n

Some people they, well, want this done / really it's their own risk, isn't it, if they have these things done?

26 dɑ́:k' pɪ́ɪɸö gʌωɪŋ blʌ́nd
    Dark people going blond.

27 jɛ́:ᵊs sɛɪ k'ɑ́:mp' bɪ bʌ́ðəd a̯ səpʌ́o̯z
    Yes, they can't be bothered I suppose.

28 ɪ? lʌ́ks əz ɪf ʃɪz æ̯d ðə pɛ́ɪn?pɒt ʌ́n ɪ? ɔ́: lə tɑ́ɪm ən a
29 wʌ́ndə wɒ?ɛ́vəɪ ɪ?s gʌ́ωnə dʌ́u tə hə̣: skɪ́n lɛɪt'ɪ ʌ́n kɪ́ɪp'
30 pʌ́tɪŋ ɔ́: læ? stʌ́f ɒn | ɪts ɹɪdɪ́kjʊləs ɹɪ́ɪlɪi ɑɪ θɪ́ŋk məsɛ́öf
    It looks as if she's had the paint-pot on it all the time
    and I wonder whatever it's going to do to her skin later on
    keep putting all that stuff on / It's ridiculous really I
    think myself.

31 dʒö mɛ́mbə sætədɛɪ wew̃ wɪ wə k'ʌ́mɪŋ ʌp ðə ɹʌ́o̯d ɪn̯ n̯ə k'ɑ́: ən
32 ɑɪ sɛ́d ɑɪ θɔ́:t ɪ? wəz ðʌ́o̯z: pɪ́ɪpö fɹəm ɪ́ɪsbɔ:n
    Do you remember Saturday when we were coming up the road in
    the car and I said I thought it was those people from East-
    bourne?

33 ɪ? wʊ́z zɛ́m jö nʌω
    It was them you know.

34 ɑ sɛ́d ðæ? lʌ́?t lɑɪ́k | ðɪ́ɪz tʌ́u wɔ́:kɪw̃ we ðə lɛ́ɪdɪi wəz ɒ́ ðə
35 pɛ́ɪvmənᵈ ən̯ n̯ə hʌ́zbənd lʌ́k lɑɪ́k ɪn | ɑɪ hæ?nt sɪ́ɪn əm fɔ
36 s:ɪ́kʃ jɪ́iəz | nʌω kɔ́:s ɪd ɪ́znt
    I said that looked like / these two walking, well, the lady
    was on the pavement and the husband looked like him / I
    hadn't seen them for six years / No, course it isn't.

37 ɛ́nɪwɛɪ wɪ fɑ́o̯n̯ n̯ɪs nʌ́ot wew̃ wɪ gʊɾ ɪ́n
    Anyway we found this note when we got in.

38 ɪ?ʃ jɔ́:ᵊ hɑ́ωs ɪ̯zn̯ ɪ?
    It's your house, isn't it?

39 ɑ dɪdn ʌndəstǽ:mb wɑ́ɪ ʃɪ sɛ́d ʃɪ kədn:? lɛ́t ə: lʌ́k æt ɪt |
40 sə bɪ́? sɪ́lɪi ɹɪ́ᵊlɪi | wö ðæ?s dɑ́:fp bɪkəz ɪ?s nʊ́? dəzn?
41 bɪlʌ́ŋ tə ðɪ ɛ́ɪdʒən: ɪ?s ɛ́: hɑ́ωs

55

I didn't understand why she said she couldn't let her look at it / It's bit silly really / Well, that's daft, because it's not doesn't belong to the agent, it's her house.

42 ʃɪ wɒnʔtəd mɪi tə sénɲ ɲɪs télɪgɹǽːm tə ðəm | waɪ aɪ ʃb
43 wéɪsʔtˀ mʌ́nɪi ɒn télɪgɹǽːmz ən θɪŋz laɪʔ ðǽːt

She wanted me to send this telegram to them / Why I should waste money on telegrams and things like that.

44 kös zə létəz ədˀ bɹiŋ kɹɒ́sɪŋ ɪɲ ɲə pʌ́ɷst

'Cos the letters had been crossing in the post.

45 ɑ wəz dʒǽːst jə nʌɷ dóʊɪŋ͡nə mɪ́iɫ əɲ fʌ́ɷw̃ wɛ́nʔ nɛ́ks dɔ́ə ɲ̥
46 ɲɛɪ kɛ́ɪm əž sɛ́d ɔ ɪts fə jóʊ

I was just you know doing the meal and [the] phone went next door and they came and said, Oh, it's for you.

47 dɪd vɪ́k hæv ə | sʊ́f twɪ́id hǽt ɒn ɔ sʌ́mθɪŋʔ laɪʔ lǽːʔ | wɒ
48 lóʊkɪŋ aɷʔ ðə kɑ́ː aɪ sɛ ɪʔ lóʊʔ sʌ́mθɪŋʔ laɪʔ lǽːʔ | ʃɪ sɛd wɨ
49 áɪ hæd ə bɹǽɒn pɪ́nɪfɔə dɹɛs

Did Vic have a / soft tweed hat on or something like that? / Well, looking out of the car, I said, it looked something like that. / She said, Well, I had a brown pinafore dress.

50 sʌɷ ʃɪi sɛ wɪi kˀɔ́ŋʔ gɛʔ nɪi ɑ́ːnsə fɹəm ɲɪs háɷs

So she said, We couldn't get any answer from this house.

51 ɛ́nɪwɛɪ ʃɪ sɛd wɪi poʊ̃ fɪ́ftɹɪ pǽɒnz daɷn ɒɲ ɲə lɑ́ːs bʌ́ŋgəlʌɷ
52 ðəʔs tə bɪ bɪ́ɫʔ lɛ́ə

Anyway she said, We put fifty pounds down on the last bungalow that's to be built there.

53 ɪʔs tɪ́pɪkɫ ɒv əm ðeɪ ɔ́ː lə sɛ́ɪm | nʌɷ dɪ́fɹɲʔ fəɪ ɛ́nɪwʌn
54 ɛ́öɫs

It's typical of them, they're all the same / No different for anyone else.

55 sǽtədeɪ hɹɪ ɹʌ́ŋ | djoʊ mɑ́ɪnd ɪf aɪ stɛ́ɪ nɛks wɪ́ik

Saturday he rung / Do you mind if I stay next week?

56 mʌs bɪi dífɪkö? ɹíilɪi mʌ́sn̩ ɪ?

Must be difficult really, mustn't it?

57 wǫ́ leɪ dʌö̃? wö́? mɪi tə líiv jét əwaɪɫ | θíŋk ðɛv bɪn lívɪn
58 ɪɾ ʌ́p ə bɪt ðɪs lɑ́:st wíik̚ | wént tω ə k'ʌ́pl əv dɑ́:z̃ɪz jω
59 nʌ́ω

Well, they don't want me to leave yet awhile. / Think
they've been living it up a bit this last week. / Went to
a couple of dances, you know.

60 ðɪ́s wɪik hɪiz gɒ́t̚ tə gʌ́ω tə skʊ́?lənd | sʌ̃́θɪŋk tə dóu wɪ ðə
61 fə̣́:m

This week he's got to go to Scotland / something to do with
the firm.

62 a̱ dʌ́ɒn wóne wʌ́ɹɪ jou | méɪkɪn ə bíg̚ dʒɒ́b

I don't want to worry you / making a big job.

(iv) *Phonological discussion*
The most important characteristics of C's speech are:
the /ɒ/-/ʌ/ distinction, no syllable-final /r/, consistent use of /h/, unstressed, word-final /ɪi/. [ŋ]
occurs without a following [g] more than in Stockport;
see below for details. The commonest processes are
harmony and CCS.

(a) *Lenition*. The bilabials appear to be those
sounds that are particularly subject to lenition, e.g.

[ʌɸ] *up* (18)
[pɪiɸö] *people* (26)
[a̰ũ] *I'm* (13).

In the last example, the lenition has gone from stop
to vocoid. There is also frequent vocalization of
/l/ in word-final or pre-consonantal position, e.g.

[stɪö] *still* (3)
[pɪiɸö] *people* (26)
[pɪipö] *people* (32)
[məsɛöf] *myself* (30).

There are, however, exceptions to this, e.g.

[waɪɫ] *while* (17)

[pɪipɫ̩] *people* (17).

The other frequent type of lenition is intervocalic voicing of /t/

[ɪd̥ ɪʔ] *it it* (7) (with partial voicing only)

[ɪd ɪznt] *it isn't* (36).

There is also a tendency to flap such consonants, e.g.

[gɒɾ ɪn] *got in* (37).

(b) *Harmony*. The alveolars /t d n/ harmonize their place of articulation to a following consonant, e.g.

[əbaʊp̂ʔ maɪ] *about my* (12)

[kʻɑːmp̂ʔ bɪ] *can't be* (27)

[ʌndəstæːmb waɪ] *understand why* (39)

[dɑːfp̂ bɪkəz] *daft because* (40)

[ʃb wɛɪsʔt] *should waste* (42-43)

[pɒʈ̂ʔ fɪftɪi] *put fifty* (51)

[dɪfɪʧʔ fəɹ] *different for* (53)

[əbaʊt̪̂ ðɪiz] *about these* (17).

Although place harmony is usual, there are examples where it does not occur, e.g.

[pɛɪnʔpɒt] *paint-pot* (28).

In the case of syllabic nasals there are dual articulations, as in

[hæpm͡n̩d] *happened* (21).

There are also a number of examples of manner harmony, with place harmony as well, as appropriate, e.g.

[ʌʊ̃ ɹɪsk] *own risk* (24)

[wɛ̃w̃ wɪ] *when we* (31) and (37)

[əz̃ sɛd] *and said* (46).

There is a left-to-right nasal harmony of [nd]-sequences, whether /nd/ originally, or derived from /nt/ by voicing (lenition), e.g.

[ɹaʊ̃nː] *round* (3)

[ɛɪdʒə̃nː] *agent* (41).

The derivation of the latter form is thus:

/ɛɪdʒənt/

Voicing ⇒ ɛɪdʒənd

Nasal harmony ⇒ [ɛɪdʒənː].

This harmony does not always take place, as can be seen from a form such as [pɛɪvmənd] *pavement* (35). There is one context where the harmony affects two following segments: /nd ð/, as in:

/sɛnd ðɪs/

Nasal harmony ⇒ sɛnn ð̃ɪs

ð harmony ⇒ sɛnn nɪs

Place harmony ⇒ [sɛn̪n̪ n̪ɪs] (42).

In rapid speech Geminate Simplification takes place; this is particularly common with the negative ending of auxiliary verbs, e.g.

[wɒn̩] *wouldn't* (22)

[ɪ̩zn̩] *isn't* (38).

The disappearance of the final /t/ is not caused by CCS, because such cases may be followed by either a consonant or a vowel. (The above examples are both followed by a vowel.)

/m/ harmonizes occasionally to a following consonant, as in [sɪind] *seemed* (7). This may be further subject to CCS with nasality left on the preceding vowel (see below), e.g. [sʌ̃θɪŋk̚] *something* (60). Nasalization of the preceding vowel occurs occasionally before /n/, e.g. [wɒ̃nʔtəd] *wanted* (42).

Palatal harmony is common:

[ɔːwɪʒ jɒus] *always used* (1)

[ɹɒuɪndʒə] *ruined your* (21)

[sːɪikʃ jɹiəz] *six years* (36)

[ɪʔʃ jɔːᵊ] *it's your* (38),

though there are instances where it has not applied, e.g.

[djɒu] *do you* (55).

/ð/-harmony is likewise widespread. (There are no examples of /θ/-harmony.)

[wɛɫ lɪ] *well the* (7)

[ən̪ n̪æʔs] *and that's* (15)

[ðæːʔs sə] *that's the* (23)

[æv vɪiz] *have these* (25)
[wɒn̥ʔ n̥ɪs] *want this* (24)
[kös zə] *'cos the* (44)
[bɪɫʔ lε̞ə] *built there* (52).

A common example of this harmony operating at a greater distance, over three segments, is [lɑɪʔ læːʔ] *like that* (47) and (48). We may note that /l/-vocalization must take place after /ð/-harmony, e.g.

/wεl ðεɪ/

/ð/-harmony ⇒ wεɫ lεɪ

/l/-vocalization ⇒ [wö̞ lεɪ] (57).

(UVD also operates on *well* in this case.) Geminate Simplification also applies in some instances after /ð/-harmony, e.g. [ɔː læʔ] *all that* (30).

One particular example, which is rather unusual, has quite a complex derivation:

/ænd ðɪi fʌɷn/

Stress placement	⇒	ənd ðə fʌɷn
Place harmony	⇒	ən̪d ðə fʌɷn
CCS	⇒	ən̪ ðə fʌɷn
/ð/-harmony	⇒	ən̪ n̪ə fʌɷn
UVD	⇒	ən̪ n̪ fʌɷn
Geminate simplification	⇒	[ən̪ fʌɷw̃] (45).

(Place and manner harmony have applied to the final nasal in this instance.) The fact that it is unusual is no doubt reflected by the number of processes that have operated. Furthermore, there may well be some kind of constraint on the number and/or type of rules that can apply in any one derivation. In this case the original /n/ of *and* has not harmonized again to the following /f/, as it would do if there were no definite article, as in, for example, *and phone him*. Harmony has operated twice in this derivation; perhaps a third occurrence is ruled out.

(c) *CCS*. CCS operates, as in most accents, on /t/ and /d/:

[dʒʌs kɷdn̩ʔ] *just couldn't* (4)
[sɪim tə] *seemed to* (8)
[lɷʔ sʌmθɪŋʔ] *looked something* (48)

[kʊŋʔ] *couldn't* (50)

[paɒnz] *pounds* (51).

The oral closure of /n/ is deleted with nasality on the preceding vowel, e.g.

[mãɪz vɛɹɪi] *mine's very* (6)

[dʌɒ̃ʔ θĩʔ] *don't think* (6)

[õ ðə] *on the* (34).

Thus, with *don't* in particular, we find either [dʌɒ̃ʔ] or a derivation with Voicing, Nasal Harmony and Geminate Simplification (see above), giving [dʌɒn], as in [dʌɒn wɒnə] *don't want to* (62). There are no examples of /n/-deletion in such words (cf. Stockport above), that is forms such as *[dʌɒʔ] do not occur (but cf. Wells, 1982: 318, who gives the form [dᶻʌʔnʌːᵁ], *don't know*, though this may be untypical).

The sequence /ng/ is always realized as [ŋ] at a morpheme boundary, as in standard English (cf. Chomsky and Halle, 1968: 85). This means a /g/-deletion rule operating on this environment after place harmony of /n/ has occurred. Alternatively, it would be possible to treat such forms in the same way as the [nd]⇒[n] forms, which also only occur at morpheme boundaries, e.g. [dʌɒn] *don't* (62), but not *[wʌnə] *wonder*. These forms involve left-to-right Voicing, left-to-right Nasal Harmony and Geminate Simplification, which could apply to words like *sing* too:

		/kaːnt/	/sɪng/
Voicing	⇒	kaːnd	———
Alveolar Harmony	⇒	———	sɪŋg
L-to-R N Harmony	⇒	kaːnn	sɪŋŋ
Geminate Simplif.	⇒	[kaːn]	[sɪŋ].

(At some stage in the history of English this process eliminated the final /b/ from words such as *lamb*.)

The present participle ending has both the /-ɪng/ and the /-ɪn/ suffix. It is perhaps significant that only the former occurs at the beginning of the conversation, whereas the latter appears also later on, e.g. [lɪvɪn] *living* (57), [mɛɪkɪn] *making* (62). This may indicate that the informant is conscious of being recorded to start with, but settles down after a few minutes. The words ending in unstressed *-thing*, e.g. *something*, have either [-ɪŋʔ] or [-ɪŋ]. The former seems to occur when the following sound has a contoid articulation, e.g.

[sʌmθɪŋʔ lɑɪʔ] (47) and (48)
[sã̃θɪŋ̊k tə] (60) (with velar closure as well),
but [ɛnɪθɪŋ ɪf sʌmθɪŋ hæpm̂nd] (20-21).
(Wells, 1982: 317, suggests that the form underlying *something*, and, presumably, all the other words ending in unstressed *-thing*, ends in /-θɪŋk/. Whilst this may be the case for some broader London speech-types, in C's speech the [ʔ] with or without a simultaneous velar closure is epenthetic rather than underlying.)

(d) *UVD*. There are a number of examples of UVD which are commonly found in most varieties of colloquial spoken English, e.g.

[lɛɪt'ɪɒn] *later on* (29)

[sə] *It's a* (40)

[aɷʔ ðə] *out of the* (48)

[ʃb] *should* (42).

[ən fʌɷw̃] is discussed above. [dʒö mɛmbə] *Do you remember* (31) is also common in spoken English: the vowel of *do*, as an unstressed auxiliary verb, is deleted, and so is the first vowel of *remember*. In the latter case /r/-deletion operates as well, giving the following derivation:

/dɷu jɷu rɪmɛmbr̩/

Stress placement ⇒ dɷ jɷ rɪmémbə

UVD (x 2) ⇒ dʒörmémbə

/r/-deletion ⇒ [dʒö mémbə].

(I have omitted details irrelevant to the present discussion, e.g. Palatal Harmony.)

(e) *Linking r*. Linking r is used in most cases intervocalically, but not always, e.g.

[p'ɛɪpəɹ a] *paper I* (3)

[mɔːɹ ə] *more or* (4)

[sɛɹ ʌɷĩ] *their own* (24)

[heə ən] *hair and* (2).

There are no examples of "intrusive" r.

(f) *Vowel lengthening*. The open vowels /æ/ and /ɛ/ lengthen before a nasal consonant in a final stressed syllable; /n/ may be followed by /d/, e.g.

[hæːnd] *hand* (4)

[ɛːnd] *end* (5)

[stæːnd] *stand* (22)

[ʌndəstæːmb] *understand* (39).

This applies even when the stress is secondary rather than main, e.g. [tɛlɪgɹæːm] *telegram* (42) (and in the plural (43)). /ɛ/ does not always lengthen, e.g. [sɛn̥n̥] *send* (42), and the other vowels never do, e.g. [blɒnd] *blond* (26), [dʌn] *done* (24). Stressed *that* also tends to have a lengthened vowel phase, e.g. [ðæːt̬] (43).

Chapter Three

PEASMARSH, SUSSEX

There are two informants, both women. Informant W, aged 87, lived in Peasmarsh all her life; informant B, aged 64, was born at nearby Sellindge but moved to Peasmarsh in her teens and has lived there ever since.

(i) *General*
Both speakers have a relatively tense musculature. The voiceless stops are only weakly aspirated initially, /t/ more than the other two. /r/ is post-alveolar and following consonants, which are alveolar elsewhere, have a tendency to be post-alveolar too (see below under Harmony).

Lip-rounding is produced without protrusion and is most apparent in [ɔː], [ɵ] and [ɶ]. In the other vocoid articulations lip-position varies from spread to neutral. Speaker B sometimes has slight lip-rounding in the initial phase of the diphthong in *time* [ʊɪ].

(ii) *Vowel diagrams*
I have put both speakers on the same diagrams, as they are for the most part the same. B regularly has three different articulations, which I have bracketed on the diagrams.

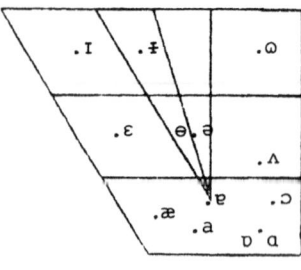
short monophthongs

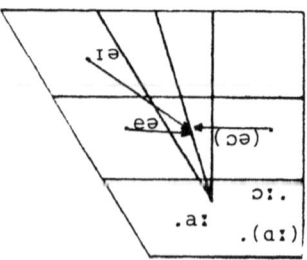
long monophthongs and centralizing diphthongs

64

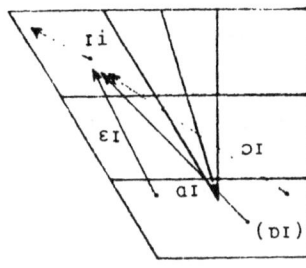
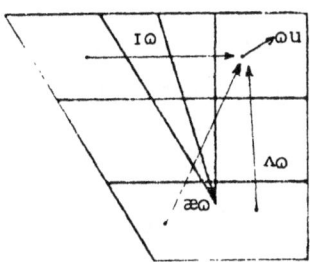

front closing diphthongs back closing diphthongs

(iii) *The transcription of speaker W*

1 ʔɛ́ɪwɔɹdn̥ ǽʊs ɪʔ wəz kɔ́ːɫd | jɪ́ɹz əgʌʊ | bʌt aɪ θɪ́ŋg̊ ɪʔs
2 kɔ́ːɫd sʌ́mθɪŋ ɛ́ɫs næʊ

  Hawarden House it was called / years ago / but I think it's called something else now.

3 ðɪ ʌ́ʊɫd fæʃnn neɪm wəz ɛ́ɪwɔɹdn̥ | ðætʼ kɒ́tɪdʒ

  The old-fashioned name was Hawarden / that cottage.

4 ʃɪi njʊ́ʊ wɛn ɪʔ wəz gɔ́ɪnə ɹɛ́ɪn | wɛ́n ʃɪ wəz dɔ́ʊɪŋ kɔ́ɹsɪts |
5 ən ʃɪ jʊ́ostʼə lɛ́ɪ əɹ kɔ́ɹsɪts dǽɔn pɒ́d̥ əɹ ǽ·nᵈz ɒ̈n̥ ðə tɛ́ɪbɫ
6 n gʌ́ʊ ɔ·f tə slɪ́ip

  She knew when it was going to rain / when she was doing corsets / and she used to lay her corsets down put her hands on the table and go off to sleep.

7 wɛ́n ʃɪ wəz mǽɹɪd ʃɪ wəz wɜɹkɪŋ fə mɪ́stəɹ fɪ́ɫməɹ | ðə
8 glʌ́vɹɪ | glʌ́vz ən lɛ́gɪnz ən spǽts əz ðeɪ jʊ́ostə kɔ́ːɫ ɫəm

  When she was married she was working for Mister Filmer / the glovery / Gloves and leggings and spats as they used to call them.

9 ðɛɪ stáɹtɪd ɪm wáɪtnáɪts | ðə mɪ́dɫ ǽʊs əv ðʌ́ʊs θɹɪ́i

  They started in Whiteknights / the middle house of those 3.

65

10 ʃiɪ dɪdn wɜ́ɪk fəɪ énibaɪɪ
   She didn't work for anybody.

11 ɐ spöoz ɪ? wɔ́·z | aɪ ka·n ɹ́ivn̩ ɹɪmémbɹ ɪ dóuɪŋ əm | ʌóni
12 ðət ʃɪi díd' dou əm
   I suppose it was / I can't even remember her doing them /
   only that she did do them.

13 ɹáɪt ʌp ? ðə táp əv ðə stɹɨ́it˺
   Right up at the top of the street.

14 maɪ fá·ðəɪ ɪz níəɪɪs ðə fén˘s | maɪ mʌ́ðəɪ ən aɪ əɪ ə̥t ðə
15 geɪt
   My father is nearest the fence / My mother and I are at the
   gate.

16 ʌ́oni dʒʌ́st ə péɪvmɨn? nǽɪöo péɪvmɨn? bɪtwíiŋ n̥ë hǽos ən n̥ë
17 | féns
   Only just a pavement narrow pavement between the house and
   the fence.

18 dǽɒn ɛgzɔ́ʷɫ | bádm əv ðə hɪ́ɫ | ən θɹíi p'ɫ́ɪismən ǎn͡m pɔ́ɪnt˺
19 dɹ́uti | ən maɪ vá·ðəɪ sɛd ə | ɪ? wəz əβǽo? mídnaɪt' | sʌ́o
20 áɪ æd t'ə gʌ́o wɪð ɪm ë_ɛ́ɫp' p'ʊ́ʃ ðə ǧaɪt | dʒʌ́ss ə t'óu
21 wɹ́iɫd tɹʌ́k laɪk | köɪs zə k'áfɪm wəz kʌ́vəɪd ʌ́·p' | əz jóuʒə
22 | wɛ́m wɹi gát˺ dǽɒn də ðə báɹm əv ɛ́gzʌɒɫ ?ɪ́ɫ ðɛ wəɪ θɹíi
23 p'ɫ́ɪismən ǎn͡m pɔ́ɪnt˺ dɹ́ut'ɪ | ænd maɪ vá·ðəɪ séd˺ t'o əm ɪts
24 ɔ́ː ɹáɪ? wɹiv gád̥ ə lǽ·ntəɪn bəd ɪts bǽk ʌp ðə ɹʌ́od
   Down Eggshole / bottom of the hill / and three policemen on
   point duty / and my father said er / it was about midnight
   / so I had to go with him er help push the cart / Just a
   two-wheeled truck, like / 'Course the coffin was covered up
   / as usual / When we got down to the bottom of Eggshole
   Hill, there were three policemen on point duty / and my
   father said to them it's all right, we've got a lantern but
   it's back up the road.

25 ?ǽd tə ɪŋ n̥ə féɪs wɜ́ɪɫd wɔ́ɪ kəz ɔ́ːɫ ɪz mɛ́n wə kɔ́ːɫd ʌ́·p |
26 ðɛn aɪ ǽd˺ tə bɪ bɔ́ɪ | gɹáɪn̥n̥ n̥ə wáɪ? léd nd ðə ɹéd léd fə

27 ðə pɛɪnʔ | mɪ́ks ʌp ðə pʌ́tɪi ən sʌtʃ lɑɪk | s·g̊ɪɑ́ɪnd ɪt ʌ́p
28 ət ðǽtʔ tɑ́ɪm ə dɛɪ kəz ɪʔ jóus̥ kʻʌ́m ɪn ə bɪ́g̊ kʻɛ́g | ɪ́n̥ n̥ðə
29 pɛ́ɪnt | jə ɑdʔ tə gɪɑ́ɪnd ɪd̥ ʌ́p kəz ɪt̪p wəz lɑ́ɪk:ˑklɑ́g̊g̊
30 təgɛ́ðəɪ jə sɪ́i

Had to in the First World War 'cos all his men were called up / Then I had to be boy / Grind the white lead and the red lead for the paint / mix up the putty and such like / Used to grind it up at that time of day 'cos it used to come in a big keg / In the paint / you had to grind it up 'cos it was like clogged together, you see.

31 jou ɑdʔ tʻə mɪ́ks ɪt ʃəsɛ́ɫf

You had to mix it yourself.

32 ɪ́i wəz bɔ́ɪn̥ ðɛ ɪn ə sɛ́ɪm ɪoum ɑ́ɪ wəz bɔ́ɪn̥ ɪn

He was born there in the same room I was born in.

33 ðə fɛ́ɪs lɑɾ ə bǽʃfəɪdz̥ lɪ́vd ɪn: | wɛ́ɪ mɑɪ gɪǽm̥vəɪ lɪ́vv̥ |
34 ɪn̥ n̥ǽʔ kɔ́ɪnɪ ǽɒs

The first lot of Bashfords lived in / where my granfer (= grandfather) lived / in that corner house.

35 jóu kn̥ ɪɪmɛ́mbɪ əm ðɛ́əɪ

You can remember them there.

36 wʊ́z ɪʔ ʔmɑ́ɪd ə bɪ́n

Was it? It might have been.

37 ðɛɪ dɑ́ɪd ɔ́:f

They died off.

38 ən̥ ðə ʔǽɒs wəz dʒəs lɛ́f tə ɪóuɪnz̥

And the house was just left to ruins.

39 ɫi lɪ́vd əd ə sɔ́ɪd̥ əv ə gɛ́ɪtʻ | ə lɪdɫ bʌ́ŋgɫʌ̃ɒ ɔ̃ɫ ɑn ɪz ʌ́ɒn
40 | fɪ́ɫθɪi dɛ́ɪtʻɪi ʌɒɫ mǽ:n

He lived at a sort of a gate / a little bungalow all on his own / filthy dirty old man.

41 ɪ jóus tə wɛ́ɪç f ɛ́nɪbʊdɪ əd ɪmpˈlɔ́ɪ ɪ̥m | bət nʌ́ɒbᵊdɪ áɪdlɪ
42 wɔ́d: ɪmpˈlɔ́ɪ ɪ̥m

He used to work for anybody who'd employ him / but nobody hardly would employ him.

43 ɪtp wɔ́d⌐ bɹ̵i

It would be.

44 wɛ̝ᵊ maɪ sístɹɪnlɔ́: lívv ðæd ǽʊs ɪz dǽɒn tə ðə gɹǽɒn

Where my sister-in-law lived, that house is down to the ground.

45 wɪ ad ən ɔ́ɪgənɪss fɹəm ɹáɪ | ən əɪ fɹɛ́nn | əņ ðɛ́ņ ʃɹi wez̥
46 tˈɒk ít wɪð ə nɛ́ɪvəs bɹɛ́ɪkʰdæɒn

We had an organist from Rye / and her friend / and then she was took ill with a nervous breakdown.

47 ðə víkəɪ | wʌ́ndəɪz if jɒu kʊd ɛ́ɬp ǽʊ? wɪð ðə | fɛ́ɪs láɪn
48 əv ɛ́vɹɪ ím

The vicar / wonders if you could help out with the / first line of every hymn.

49 aɪv nɛ́vəɪ tʌ́tʃt ə ɔ́ɪgən ɪn mɪ láɪf | aɪ dʌnɒ ʔɛ́nɪθɪn əbæɒd
50 ən ɔ́ɪgən | ən aɪ dʌ́ɒn? θɪ́ŋk ʔǽt nʌ́ɒz ɛ́nɪθɪŋ əbæɒ? mí̵i

I've never touched a organ in my life / I don't know anything about an organ / and I don't think that knows anything about me.

51 ɪi sɛd w jɔ́u tɔ́:g ɪd ʌ́ɒvə wɪð ǽɹɪi wɛn ɪi kʌ́mz̥ ɪn tə lʌ́ntʃ

He said, Well, you talk it over with Harry when he comes in to lunch.

52 ɪi stáɪtɪd ɔ:f bǽk⌐ tˈə wɛ́ɪk | əm bǽk ɪi kʌ́m | ɪi sɛ́d wɛ́ɬ |
53 pɹǽpʃ jɒud⌐ gɛt θɹóu ðǽ·t⌐ | sʌɒ ɔ́:f ʌp ðə víkəɪz aɪ wɛ́n? | ɪi
54 wez̥ | ʌ́p⌐ táps kəz aɪd⌐ gɔ́:n ʌp ? sí̵i ɪm | ən aɪ ǽt ? gɒ ...
55 ʔɔl θɹɒu ðɹi ímz̥ ɒn ə blóumɪn ᴨɪǽnʌɒ

He started off back to work / and back he come / He said, Well / perhaps you'd get through that / So off up the vicar's I went / He was / up tops 'cos I'd gone up to see him / and I had to go ... all through the hymns on a blooming piano.

68

(iv) *The transcription of speaker B*

56 ʃɹi æd ə ʃɒ̃k̚ dídn̩ ʃíi
    She had a shock, didn't she?

57 1ʔ jǿus ʔ bḭ ɹíilɪ wʌ́ndəfɫ dǿu ɹíilɹi | ənd évɹɪweɹ dʒɔ́ɪnd
58 íːn | ɔ́ːɫ ðə víliʤɪz | jǿus tˈ æv ɔ́ːɫ dɹés káɹts
    It used to be really wonderful do, really / and everywhere joined in / all the villages / used to have all dressed carts.

59 wɪ jǿus tə gʌ́ω ɹǽωṇṇ ðə dífɹən ǽωzɪz̥
    We used to go round the different houses.

60 wɹ́i jωus tə bɪ síŋɪŋ wʌ́n énn əð ðə bǽːnn wəz̥ plέɪɪŋ ðɹi
61 ʌ́ðəɹ énd ʒω nʌ́ω
    We used to be singing one end and the band was playing the other end, you know.

62 wɪ jωus tə stáːtˈ ɔ́ːf | wʌ́n ǽωs wɒd ə ént'ət'έɪn əs |
63 wɪ jωus t æv ɹʌ́m pʌ́ntʃ ən ... ɔ́ː sɔ·ts ə lɪɫ snǽks ɪn̩ ðéəɹ
    We used to start off / one house would er entertain us / We used to have rum punch and ... all sorts of little snacks in there.

64 wɪ ɔ́ːɫ went ɪnd̥ɔ́əz əv kɔ́əs z̰ sǽʔ n̩ n̩ə dɹɔ́ːɪŋ ɹωumz ən díd
65 εəɹ síŋɪn | ən táɪm wɪ gɒtˈ hʌ́ωm wii wəz véɹɪ méɹɪi jω nʌ́ω
    We all went indoors, of course, and sat in the drawing rooms and did our singing / and time we got home, we was very merry, you know.

66 wɪ jωus tə síŋ ɔ́ːɫ lə weɪ hʌ́ωm bət ná? kǽɹəɫz
    We used to sing all the way home, but not carols.

67 wɪ jωus t ǽv mʌ́ωst ɪnʤɔ́ɪəbö tɒ́ɪm
    We used to have (a) most enjoyable time.

68 wɒ́nt ʃωu ɪn̩ n̩ə tˈɹ́im
    Wasn't you in the team?

69

69 ðæts ɔ:° dɪ́d ǽɒt nɑ́ω
   That's all died out now.

70 lʌ́ndənəɪz bɪ́ɪ ə ... ǽv və kɑ́dɪdʒɪz fə wíikénd
   Londoners buy er ... have the cottages for (a) week-end.

71 ðεn nǽʔ míinz zə píipɬ θuv | gɑ́d ə gʌ́ω ɪntə ðə kǽɒnsɬ ɑ́ωzɪz
   Then that means the people who've (?) / got to go into the council houses.

72 sέvəm pǽɒɲψ fəɪ s̲ɪ́ɪi bέdɪoum
   Seven pound for three bedroom ...

73 ðë vέɪɪi nɑ́ɪs | kəs zəz nɑ́ʔ mεnɪi vɑ́ɪm kɑ́tɪdʒɪz nǽω ɪz zə
   They're very nice. / 'Course there's not many farm cottages now, is there?

74 kəs zʌ́ωz kɑ́tɪdʒɪz dǽɒɲ ðə bɒ́dəm ðε̞ɪ wɒʔ wə́:ɪ vɑ́ɪm kɑ́tɪdʒʃ
75 bɪn sʌ́ωɬd ǽvn nέɪ
   'Course those cottages down the bottom there what were farm cottages (have) been sold, haven't they?

76 ðεɪ tɑ́ʔ ðə θǽtʃ ɑ́v əm pɒ́ʔ ðə slέɪtʼ ɒn dídn ðεɪ
   They took the thatch off and put the slate on, didn't they?

77 ɪf jω gʌ́ω tə síi əɪ hə́:ɪ hǽÿs ɪz ən ʌ́ωɬd θǽtʃt hɑ́ωs
   If you go to see her, her house is an old thatched house.

78 ʃɪ jόustʼ tə lív ət ðə tɑ́p ə ðə stɪɪ́it
   She used to live at the top of the street.

79 skʌ́ωɬ lέɪn wəz dɪέdfö weŵ wɪ wέnt | ʔ wz ɔ́:° pʊ́thʌω:z | ɪ̲ʔ
80 wz ʌ́ωnlɪ wεn nə wɔ́: kέɪm ðəʔ ðεɪ mέɪd ðə ɪʌ́ωd ʌp
   School Lane was dreadful when we went. / It was all pot-holes. / It was only when the war came that they made the road up.

81 ðέn ðεɪ dɪsɪ́dɪd tə mέɪk ðə ɪʌ́ωd ʌp wɪ ðɪ ɑ́:ᴵmɪi
   Then they decided to make the road up with the Army.

82 kɔs wɪ jóʊs t æv ə fɔ́ɹdʒ íəɹ ə gǿd mɛnɪ jíəɹz ən nǽʊ ɪʔs
83 klǿz dá·ɒn | wɪtʃ wəz̥ ɹá:ðəɹ ə ʃǽ·ɪm ɑɪ θí:ŋk

'Course we used to have a forge here a good many years and now it's closed down / which was rather a shame, I think.

84 ðɪi ə sʊ́ɪkɫ ʃɒ́p jʊʊs ə βɪ ɑn̩ n̩ɪ ʌ́ðə sɑɪd ðə ɹə́ʊd

The er cycle shop used to be on the other side (of) the road.

85 vɛ́ɹɪ ʌʊɫd místə vá:ɹlë lívˬ ðëɪ | ðə vá:ðəɹ əv ɔ́: ðʌʊz̥

Very old Mr Farley lived there / the father of all those.

86 ą̈ ʃt θíŋk sʌʊ jɛ́:

I should think so, yes.

87 ðə wəz ǿnlɪ bʌ́s wɛnʔ twɑ̈ɪs ə wíik

There was only (a) bus went twice a week.

88 wɛ́nzdɪ̩ má:ɹkɪtˀ déɪ ǽnd ɑ́n: ə sǽtədɛ̩ɪ

Wednesday market day and on er Saturday.

89 ðɛɪ wz wʌ́ndəfö | bət ɪf ðə dɹʊ́ɪvəɹ wʊ́nɪd ʔ pʊp ín n æv ɪz̥
90 t'íi jö jʊʊs t'æv də wɛ́ɪʔ fə hím jʊ síi

They was wonderful / But if the driver wanted to pop in and have his tea, you used to have to wait for him, you see.

91 ɑ:ftə ə̥ fə́ɹs wéɹl wɔ́:ᵊɹ | ᵊwəz̥ nʌ́ʊ tɹɑ́:z̥spɒ·ʔ wɒʔsʌʊɛ́vʌ

After the First World War / there was no transport whatsoever.

92 i mɑɪd ə gɑd ə bɑ́ɪk sʌ́ɪkɫ

You might have got a bike, cycle.

93 ɪʔ wəz ə vɛ́ɹɪi pɔ́:ɹ ʌʊɫ plɛ̩́ɪs wɛw̃ wɹi fə́ɹs kɛ̩́ɪm híʌ

It was a very poor old place when we first came here.

94 ðə wəz nʌʊ wɔ́:təɹ ï̩ɲ ŋ̊ǽʔ hǽʊs ɑ̈ɪ ɛ́nɪθɪŋ | wɪ ǽdˀ də fʊ́ɪnd ə
95 spɹɪ́ŋ ǽʊtˀ ɪŋ ðə wʊ́dˀ də gɛd ɛʊ wɔ́:tə́ᴵ

There was no water in that house or anything / We had to find a spring out in the wood to get our water.

96 ɔːɫ ɛəɹ klʌ́b mémbəz

All our club members.

97 wʊ́z jɒu ðéəɹ

Was you there?

98 äv dʌ́n sʌm θíŋz ɪm mɪ tʊ́ɪm | äv lókt áːftəɹ ə pǽɹət˺

I've done some things in my time / I've looked after a parrot.

99 ən ɪʔ wʊ́zn̩ ɪn ə kɛ́ɪdʒ

And it wasn't in a cage.

100 ɪf ə jɒu wʊ́·ntɪd˺ də gɛ́d ɪd ɔ́·f ðe flɔ́ːᵊɹ ... jɒu ǽd ə pɒt˺
101 də kɛ́ɪdʒ dǽɒn fɔɹ ɪt˺ də klɑ́ɪm an

If you wanted to get it off the floor ... you had to put the cage down for it to climb on.

(v) *Phonological discussion*
Both speakers have the /ɒ/-/ʌ/ distinction, sporadic use of /h/, unstressed word-final /ɪi/ (though not in all instances), and syllable-final /r/, though there are instances of its disappearance in B's speech (see below). [ŋ] occurs without a following [g].

(a) *Lenition*. The voiceless stops and fricatives, which are otherwise fortis, are given lenis articulations, either voiced or voiceless, usually between voiced sounds, e.g.

[mɑɪd ə] *might have* (36) and (92)

[mɑɪ va·ðəɹ] *my father* (19)

[tɔːg ɪd ʌɒvə] *talk it over* (51)

[æd də] *had to* (94).

Although there are certain common occurrences of lenition, as in *got to* and *had to*, it does not always occur: for example, B says [kɑdɪdʒɪz] for *cottages* (70), but also says it twice, (73) and (74), with [t]. In the case of /t/, speaker W sometimes uses a flap, as in [lɑɾ ə] *lot of* (33). Speaker B has one instance of lenition after a voiceless sound: [ɪt də] *it*

to (101).
   On one occasion each speaker applies lenition to /b/ intervocalically producing a fricative:

   [əβæɷʔ] *about* (19)

   [ə βɪ] *to be* (84).

This appears to be a sporadic feature of rapid speech.
   Speaker B deletes /t/ in a few instances:

   [lɪɫ] *little* (63)

   [jɷus ə] *used to* (84)

   [æd ə] *had to* (100).

From the data in the recordings it is difficult to see what the derivation of these forms might be (other than an *ad hoc* /t/-deletion rule, which is unsatisfactory, if some other rule(s) can be invoked), though they occur in rapid articulations and are not the same as the major processes under consideration in this book. It is just possible that Geminate Simplification can be triggered by matching place features only in B's system rather than by a matched set of features: thus, in each case above we have two segments with alveolar contact, one of which is deleted. In each case it is the underlying /t/ that is deleted regardless of the order of the two segments. If such an explanation is justified, then we are dealing with an adaptation of an existing rule to remove the /t/.
   /l/ is frequently vocalized and sometimes deleted in post-vocalic and post-consonantal syllabic positions:

   [jɷuʒɷ] *usual* (21)

   [ɔ: ɹɑɪʔ] *all right* (24)

   [ɔ:] *all* (63) and (85)

   [dɹɛdfö] *dreadful* (79)

   [pʊthʌɷ:z] *pot-holes* (79).

   One interesting lenition feature is /r/-deletion. In post-vocalic position we find a number of slightly different articulations which plot stages in the disappearance of /r/; for example:

   [jɪəɹz̞] (82) retracted frictionless continuant
                  with retracted following consonant

   [mɛmbəz̞] (96) retracted consonant only

   [ɑːᶦmɪi] (81) slight continuant

>   [kɔ̢əs] (64) vocalization with non-retracted
>   consonant
>   [hɪʌ] (93) altered vowel quality
>   [stɑːt] (62))
>   [ʌðə] (84)) deletion.
>   [εω] (95)   )

All the above examples are from B; speaker W only has three instances and these are in unstressed syllables:

>   [ʃəsɛɫf] (31)
>   [wɛ̦ᵊ] (44)
>   [ʌωvə] (51).

Despite its deletion by B, both speakers have an underlying /r/ in post-vocalic position. In younger speakers, however, there is evidence to suggest that in some cases it has disappeared, the accent of these speakers being non-rhotic.

(b) *Devoicing*. The feature of final devoicing of voiced stops and fricatives in prepausal position and before voiceless sounds, which is widespread in most accents of English, occurs in the speech of both speakers even before voiced sounds, in word-final position and after /s/. All the examples in B's speech are of the verbal and plural s-endings. For example:

>   [wez̦] *was* (1), (3) and (4)
>   [kɔːɫd̦] *called* (2)
>   [bæʃfəɹdz̦] *Bashfords* (33)
>   [z̦ə] *the* (21)
>   [g̊ɹɑɪnd] *grind* (27)
>   [wəz̦] *was* (60) and (83)
>   [z̦əz̦] *there's* (73).

It is interesting to note that this goes in the opposite direction, as it were, from lenition, which is widespread in these speakers. It also appears to be restricted to the s-endings in B's speech in comparison to W's.

(c) *Harmony*. The alveolars /t d n/ display place harmony with a following consonant:

>   [k'afɪm wəz] *coffin was* (21)
>   [ət̪ ðə] *at the* (14)

74

[gɹæŋv̥əɪ] *grandfather* (33)

[sɛvəm pæɒŋψ fəɪ] *seven pound for* (72).

Sometimes the alveolar and the following place articulation are virtually simultaneous in W's speech, e.g.

[ɑ̈n͡m pʔɪnt] *on point* (18) and (23)

[ɪt͡p wəz] *it was* (29).

A syllabic /n/ will in some cases harmonize with the preceding consonant:

[ɪivn̩] *even* (11)

[kŋ̍] *can* (35).

Place and manner harmony occur occasionally: [wɛw̃ wɪ] (79) and (93).

Since /r/ is a post-alveolar frictionless continuant, it produces harmony in following alveolar consonants, e.g.

[bɔɹn̠] *born* (32)

[kɔɹn̠ɪ] *corner* (34)

[dəɪt̠'ɪi] *dirty* (40)

[fəɹs̠ wəɹl̠] *First World* (91).

This harmony does not always occur, e.g.

[staɪtɪd] *started* (52)

[kɑɪts] *carts* (58).

/r/ also appears to have an influence on adjacent front vowels, making them more centralized, e.g.

[jɨɪz] *years* (1)

[θɹɨi] *three* (9)

[vɛ̈ɹɪ] *very* (65).

This, too, does not always take place, e.g. [θɹɪi] (18) and (22). In B's speech the commonest word to show /r/-vowel harmony is *very*, which regularly has [ə] as its first vowel, even when it is stressed, as in lines (85) and (93).

The left-to-right nasal harmony displayed by informant C in the previous chapter is found in both speakers here, with and without Geminate Simplification. For example:

[fæʃnn̩] *fashioned* (3)

[gɹɑɪn̩n̩] *grind* (26)

[gɹæɷn] *ground* (44)

[fɹɛnn] *friend* (45)

[ka·n] *can't* (11)

[ɹæɷn̥n̥] *round* (59)

[ɛnn] *end* (60)

[bæːnn] *band* (60)

[dɪfɹən] *different* (59)

[wɒnɪd] *wanted* (89)

[wɒzn̩] *wasn't* (99).

There are exceptions to this process, e.g. [g̊ɹɑɪnd] (27), [ɛnd] (61). In B's speech it would appear from the data that /nt/ reduces to [n] but /nd/ does not, which suggests a different state of affairs from the one discussed in the previous chapter, where both reduce. In B's case /nd/ has the left-to-right harmony, whereas /nt/ does not. The latter seems to be another instance of the modified GS rule mentioned above, which removes a /t/ adjacent to any other alveolar consonant. In W's case the resultant [nn] from /nd/ is simplified by GS occasionally; /nt/ is subject to the modified GS rule, as in B's speech. The difference between these two informants and informant C is that there are no instances here of /nt/→[nd] (cf. previous chapter).

In W's speech in some instances /d/ and /t/ are subject to this left-to-right harmony, e.g.

[dʒʌss] *just* (20)

[klɑgg] *clogged* (29)

[lɪvv̥] *lived* (33) and (44, without devoicing)

[ɔɹgənɪss] *organist* (45).

We can see from the above that it involves both place and manner harmony.

ð-harmony, which involves both left-to-right harmony and manner harmony, is common in both speakers, e.g.

[kɔːɬ ɬəm] *call them* (8)

[köɹs z̥ə] *course the* (21)

[ɪn̪ n̪ə] *in the* (25)

[gɹɑɪn̪n̪ n̪ə] *grind the* (26)

[θɪŋk̚ ʔæt̚] *think that* (50)

[ɔːɬ lə] *all the* (66)

[æv və] *have the* (70)

[kəs zəz] *course there's* (73)

[wɛn̪ n̪ə] *when the* (80)

[pʊt də] *put the* (100-01).

θ-harmony has only one instance:

[fəɹ s̪ɪɹi] *for three* (72).

This is caused by the surrounding [r]-articulations and is not the same as in the instances discussed in Lodge (1981: 29).

In B's speech manner harmony applies to /n/ occasionally, e.g.

[əð̃ ðə] *and the* (60)

[z̃ sæʔ] *and sat* (64)

[tɹɑːz̃spɔ·ʔ] *transport* (91).

W has only one example of manner harmony which is probably just a sporadic occurrence: [wəɹç f] (41).

Voice harmony, which is not very widespread in English accents, (cf. Introduction, p. 9), appears in B's speech in [ʃt θɪŋk̬] *should think* (86) and probably in [ð fəɹs] *the first* (91).

Finally, °we find palatal harmony in both speakers, e.g.

[əʒ jouʒɒ] *as usual* (21)

[ɪt ʃəsɛɫf] *it yourself* (31)

[pɹæpʃ joud̚] *perhaps you'd* (41)

[ɛnd ʒɒ] *end you* (48)

[wɒnt ʃɒu] *wasn't you* (56)

[wɒʒ jɒu] *was you* (85).

(d) *CCS.* CCS applies to /t/ and /d/:

[nɪəɹɪs ðə] *nearest the* (14)

[dʒəs lɛf tə] *just left to* (38)

[ʌɒɫ mæːn] *old man* (40)

[dɹɛs kɑɹts] *dressed carts* (58)

[klʌɒz da·ɒn] *closed down* (83)

[lɪv ðëɹ] *lived there* (85)

[fəɹs weɹl wɔːᵊɹ] *First World War* (91).

There are no examples where /n/ is deleted in /-nt/ sequences; it would appear not to apply to these two speakers. [ŋ] can be treated as /ng/, as in Shepherd's Bush; there are the usual two forms of the present participle, in [-ɪŋ] and [-ɪn], the latter subject to harmony in the appropriate contexts. The difference can be accounted for in the order of application of the rules, e.g.

/-ɪng w-/

Alveolar harmony ⇒ -ɪŋg w-

/g/-deletion ⇒ -ɪŋ w-

as in [sɪŋɪŋ wʌn] (60);

/-ɪng ð-/

/g/-deletion ⇒ -ɪn ð-

Alveolar harmony ⇒ -ɪn̪ ð-

as in [plɛɪɪn̪ ðrɪ] (60).

(e) *UVD*. In B's speech, when there are two unstressed vowels together and one of them is [ə], the [ə] is deleted, e.g.

[jɵus tæv] *used to have* (58), (63), (67) and (82)

[ʌʘnlɪ bʌs] *only a bus* (87).

She also deletes [ə] following /w/, as in [wz] *was* (79), (80) and (89) (cf. Stockport above). In phonetic terms both [w] and [ə] are vocoid articulations and in rapid speech can easily be run together. The tongue position for the resultant articulation is roughly that of [ö], the lip-rounding being retained, but it is not a syllable nucleus, so that it can be suitably transcribed as [w]. (Where there is a preceding [ʔ], as at (79) and (80), that, too, has lip-rounding.)

[f ɛnɪbɒdɪ] (41) is W's only example of [ə]-deletion before a vowel, and here it is only possible because of a previous /r/-deletion. This may also be an explanation of B's [fə wɪkɛnd] (70).

The most common deletion of [ə] is following [ʔ]; this occurs in both speakers, e.g.

[ʌp ʔ sɪi] *up to see* (54)

[æt ʔ gɵ] *had to go* (54)

[jɵus ʔ bi̥] *used to be* (57)

[wɒnɪd ʔ pɒp] *wanted to pop* (89).

In one instance the [ə] precedes [ʔ]: [ʌp ʔ] *up at* (13).

(f) *Vowel lengthening*. Vowels in stressed syllables in lento speech are lengthened in most English accents, and there are some examples of this in the data under consideration here, e.g. [ʌ·p] (21) and (25), [θɪːŋk] (83), [da·ɒn] (83), [ʃæ·ɪm] (83). On the other hand, there is lengthening of low vowels before /n/, as in [læ·ntəɪn] (24), [gɔːn] (54), [bæːnn] (60). The lengthened vowel before voiceless fricatives, as in RP *father, class* and so on, is still apparent in *off* (6), (37), (52), (53), (62) and (100).

Chapter Four

EDINBURGH

There are two male informants: G, aged 50, who was born in Harburn, about 16 miles from Edinburgh, and moved to the city to start work, and H, aged 19, who was born and educated in Edinburgh, but moved out to Penicuik at the age of 5. As a child, G used a broad Scots dialect (cf. Wells, 1982: 393-99) quite different from his present accent. (I have added an excerpt from a poem, which he recited for me in his childhood dialect, at the end of his conversational transcription, but I shall not be concerned with it in the phonological discussion.)

(i) *General*
Both speakers use a relatively tense tongue in their articulations; as a consequence there is very little affrication of stops and the voiceless ones are not often aspirated. The apical contact, except for /θ/ and /ð/, which are dental, is normally post-alveolar. The vowel articulations have a tendency to be fairly centralized, even in stressed syllables. /l/ has either a central or back vowel colouring in all positions (cf. Wells, 1982: 411). /r/ has a wide range of articulations: trill, flap and frictionless continuant. It is usually apico-post-alveolar and, in certain contexts, voiceless. It is occasionally retroflex: in line (85) speaker H uses considerable retroflexion, giving an Ulster quality to that stretch of speech. It should also be noted that where I have written [ɾ] before another post-alveolar sound with a complete oral closure on the median line: [t d n l], we are not always dealing with a flap, since there may be no on-off movement of the tongue. In such cases we have a very short [d]-articulation. Such pairs as *curl* and *cuddle* may, in fact, be pronounced the same (though the latter may also undergo /l/-vocalization).

Lip-rounding is normally produced with protrusion; [ɒ] is sometimes produced without lip-rounding, i.e. [ɑ]. Both [e] and [ɛ] are used where other accents have a short /e/ sound, e.g. G's [edɪnbrʌh] and H's [ɛdɨnbʌrʌh]. The close variety is the same as the equivalent of what is a diphthong in many other accents, e.g. [eti] *eighty*. Most of the vowels are found in unstressed as well as stressed syllables. Speaker G has a range of [u] to [ü] realizations for /u/, the former more common, except after /j/. [ɑ] both long and short is used by G in certain instances where RP has /ɑ/. (See also Wells' comments, 1982: 403.)

Final stops are often released, even before another stop consonant; wherever the stop symbol is left without a diacritic, that stop is released, albeit weakly.

(ii) *Vowel diagrams*

Speaker G:

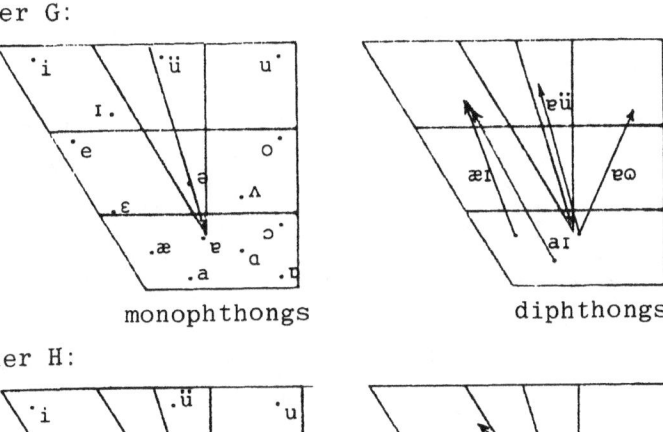

Speaker H:

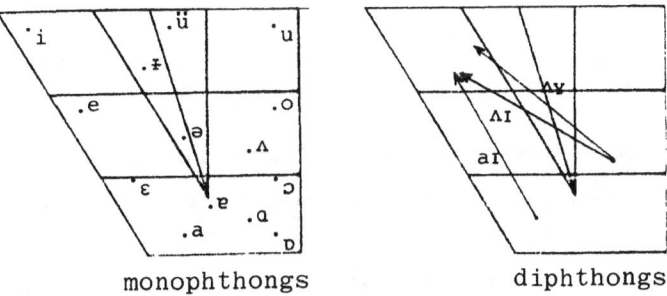

[u] is not common in H's speech, occurring only in [ɛkskɫuzɨv] (64); the front closing diphthong is sometimes [æɪ].

(iii) *The transcription of speaker G*

1 nó? nëωədez | no no onłë ðǽt wəz ðə wé wë spók ət hóm |
2 nʊ̥t ə? skúö | ? wəz wɪ̊ð ðǽt ǽksɛ̃nt ɪf jë hɐd spókən ɪn énë
3 ʌðəɾ ǽksɛnt əz ə tʃéωd | jéd əv bin łá:ft ɐot əv kóət | əz
4 pʻüt'ɪŋ ɔn éɪz ən gɾéṣëz

Not nowadays / No no only that was the way we spoke at home / not at school. / It was with that accent, if you had spoken in any other accent as a child / you'd have been laughed out of court / as putting on airs and graces.

5 ða? wəz wést kółdəɾ ë? wz ǎktʃəłë ?éütsɛɪd wést kółdəɾ ə
6 há:młët kɔłd há:ɾbʌɾn | fémas nëωədez fɪ ə gółf kóɾs

That was West Calder, it was actually outside West Calder, a hamlet called Harburn / famous nowadays for a golf course.

7 e: sɪ́kst'ʻin ɔ t'ʻe twéntë mǽɪłz

Eh sixteen or to twenty miles.

8 o jés ɪndíd | a dón? no kwǽɪt'ʻ | Mέðəɾ wɪð ðë ínɾodz əv |
9 háɪəɾ ɛdʒükéʃn n Mótnɔt ɪts méd enë dífɪəns | bət ðəz stíł
10 kwaɪt ə səbstá:nʃəö əméont əv e | ðá:t á:ksɛnt əɾéωnd

Oh yes indeed / I don't know quite / whether with the inroads of / higher education and whatnot it's made any difference / but there's still quite a substantial amount of that accent around.

11 ət skúö | o ɪf énëθɪŋ mebi ət skú wë spók słæɪ?łë póʃʌ ðən
12 wʌn téndz të dü əz wʌ́n gɛts ódəɾ

At school / oh if anything maybe at school we spoke slightly posher than one tends to do as one gets older.

13 o ðəɪ ə sévɾəł | e? ɪéndʒëz fɪəm ðə véɾë hǽɪłë ɐféktëd
14 mó:nɪŋsǽɪdˈ tü əv kɔɾθ ðə nó tɾés əv áfɛktéʃn ət óö ɪn ðə
15 püəɪ héωzɪŋ skímz

Oh, there are several / It ranges from the very highly affected Morningside to, of course, the no trace of affectation at all in the poor housing schemes.

16 kwǽɪt ə fjǘ: ənd e sʌ́m ɪá:pɪdłeʰ | gɛt ə véɾë bá:d

82

17 ɹɛpjütéʃn̥ fáˑɾ em | ə ɾʌ́f tǽɪp ténənts | nóbdë éɫs ɫ̩ gó
18 ðéəᴵ so ðë | ët éndz ʌ́pʻ wɪð ˀéˑvəbəe bɪŋ əv ðə sem tǽɪp
19 mɔɹ ə lés

Quite a few and some rapidly / get a very bad reputation
for um / er rough type tenants / nobody else'll go there
so they / it ends up with everybody being of the same type
more or less.

20 wʌn wüd ɔ́ːɫwez ɹéçəgnǽɪz ə gláːzgo áksɛnt˞ jés

One would always recognize a Glasgow accent, yes.

21 spókən | ʌ́p tü ðə tǽɪm əfː | kíŋ dʒémz ðə ë síksθ ən fʌ́ːst
22 | ᴍen hí wentʰ dëün tü íŋɫənd hi íntɹədjüst ə ɫát əv |
23 íŋɫəʃ káɾɪktəɾístɪks | ᴇm nót ən ékspeɾt əŋ n̥ǽtʰ bət̥ ðǽts
24 mǽɪ ʌndəɾstándɪŋ əv ɪt

Spoken / up to the time of King James the eh sixth and
first. / When he went down to England, he introduced a lot
of / English characteristics / I'm not an expert on that,
but that's my understanding of it.

25 ᴇ hád ə ɾʌ́stɪk ʌ́pbɾɪŋɪŋ | ᴇ wózn̩ˀ bɾɔt ʌ́p ət hóm jü si

I had a rustic upbringing / I wasn't brought up at home,
you see.

26 dɪdnˀ wʌ́ɾk an ə fáɾm bʌt e ɫívd ɪn ᴍót wəz̥ ə fómʌɾ̥
27 fáɹmhëüs

Didn't work on a farm but eh lived in what was a former
farmhouse.

28 nɔt̥ ðət ᴇm əwéɾ ɔv nó | wéɫ ɪnɫáˑnd

Not that I'm aware of, no. / Well inland.

29 am ə sívɫ séɾvənt ənd | am kɔnséɾnd wɪð ðe | ðj
30 ᴇdmínɪstɹéʃn əv ǽgɾɪkʌ́ɫtʃəɾəɫ ɫédʒɪstɫéʃn̩

I'm a civil servant and / I'm concerned with the / the
administration of agricultural legislation.

31 ðəɹ ɪz ɫéˑs dʒʌ́stɪfɪkéʃn | ə máˑhkədɫɪ dífɹənt ɫǽɪn

There is less justification / A markedly different line.

32 æɪ hæf tə gó tu ɫʌ́ndən | pɾɪ́nsɪpəlɪ tü kɔnféˑɹ wɪð kɔ́ɫigz̥
33 ɪn ɫʌ́ndən | ɔ́ɹ̝ tú e əténd əpɔ́n mæɪ mɪ́nɪstəɾ ɪf ðəz ə
34 páɫɪmént'ɹɪ dɪbét

I have to go to London / principally to confer with colleagues in London / or to eh attend upon my minister, if there's a parliamentary debate.

35 ðe ɔ́ːɫwɪz kʌm ʌ́p ət̝ ðə wɪkéˑnd

They always come up at the week-end.

36 sɔ́ ə táɾo pák ɪn̯ ðëɪ wíndo ən hɛd nɛ́vʌ sɪ́n wʌn bɪfɔ́ɹ

Saw a tarot pack in their window and had never seen one before.

37 næɪntin éti wɪɫ bɪ́ mæɪ ɾɪtǽɪɾmənt déked

1980 will be my retirement decade.

38 kɪ́pɪŋ kédʒ bʌ́ɹdz̥ | kédʒ bʌ́dz̥ əv ɔ́ɫ tǽɪps

Keeping cage birds / cage birds of all types.

39 ði ɔ́nɫi bɾɪ́dɪŋ ðət' tük plés wəz̥ pjüɾ́ɫɪ bæɪ ǽksɪdənt

The only breeding that took place was purely by accident.

40 ən éˑg fɹəm ən áːfɹɪkən sɪ́ɫvəɹ bɪ́ɫ | ðe hɛd ɫɔ́ˑts əv ʃɒ́ts
41 bɪɫ ɔ́nɫɪ wʌ́n səksés | ðə bʌ́dz v veɾɪ ʃɔ́ˑʔt ɫǽɪf ɪt səɹvǽɪvd
42 ɪts péɹənts baɪ ɔ́nɫɪ ə véɾɪ veɾ ʃɔ́ˑᵊt' tǽɪm

An egg from an African silverbill. / They had lots of shots but only one success / The birds have a very short life, it survived its parents by only a very very short time.

43 æɪ wüd əv̥ θɔ́t ʌnjüʒ́ɫ

I would have thought unusual.

44 ɔɫ̞ðo ɐv hád̯ ði ɔ́ˑd | bʌ́ɹd ɪn témpɾəɾɫe jü no ɪf ɪt wʌɹ ʔɪ́ɫ
45 əɹ sʌ́mθɪŋ ɹɛ ɪ́ndʒʌɹd

Although I've had the odd / bird in temporarily, you know, if it were ill or something or injured.

46 ə pɪ́dʒən | ə wəz̥ ə stáɹɫɪŋ əz wéɫ

84

A pidgeon / There was a starling as well.

47 ənɫéˑs sʌ́mbədɪ wónts ðəm ən téks səm wɪðɪn ə féɾɫɪ ʃóˑt˺
48 tǽɪm | ðe pút ðəm déʊ̯n ɐ θíŋk | koz ʌ́ðəwaɪz ðe wüd gét fáɹ̥
49 tü bíg ə nʌ́mbʌ

Unless somebody wants them and takes them within a fairly short time / they put them down, I think / 'cos otherwise they would get far too big a number.

50 bɐ̯ʊt nǽɪntin fóɹ̥tɪ nǽɪn

About 1949.

51 ónɫɪ kém tü édɪnbɾʌʰ | tü stáɾt wʌ́ɾk˺

Only came to Edinburgh / to start work.

52 pɾǽɪvɪt skúːz mʌ́ɹtʃənt kʌ́mpənɪ skúːz

Private schools, merchant company schools.

53 wʌn dʌ́znt síi enɪ máˑkt pɾógɾes fɹəm ðə ɹɪzʌ́ɫts

One doesn't see any marked progress from the results.

Appendix
Three stanzas of a poem in G's Scots dialect:

ə gɾét˺mʌkɫ bót˺ je mʌn bɨ̱ɫd	A great muckle boat ye mun build,
ən aɾk˺ðət kən flót˺híç ən dɾáˑɪ	An ark that can float heich an' dry,
wɨ ɾúm ɨnt˺fəɾ ɔ́ jʌɾ en fók˺	Wi' room in't for a' yer ain folk
ən háˑntoɫ o káˑtoɫ foɾbáˑɪ	An' (a) hantle o' cattle forby.
so nóaˑ ɾoxt háɾd ət̬ ðə dʒóp	So Noah wrocht hard at the job,
ən séɾtʃt të ðë ʔéɾθs fáɾðɨsp bóɾdʌɾ̥z	An' searched to the Earth's farthest borders,
ən géðəɾd̥ ðə bísts en̥ ðə bʌ́ɾdz̥	An' gethered the beasts an' the birds,
ən téɫd̥ ðəm tü stáˑn baɪ fəɾ óɾdʌɾ̥z	An' telled them to stand by for orders.

ɔ ðɨ̆s wʌzne dɨn ɔn̥ ðə kwét'   A' this wasna done on the quate,

ən níbʌr̥z wüd ʍaɪɫz geðər rún   An' neebours would whiles gether roun';

ðɛn nóa wüd dɾáp ðəm ə hɨ́nt   Then Noah would drap them a hint

laɪk'ðə wḛ́ðəɾ ɨz gón tə bɾek dṷn   Like: "The weather is gaun to break doun".

(iv) *The transcription of speaker H*

54 ðəɾ ɨz ə çjü•dʒ kómpleks ë ʃópɨn séntʌɾ | ɨʔs bin ɔɫ bɨ́ɫʔ
55 ʌ́p ɨn̥ n̥ə sén?ʌɾ ə ðə sɨ́ʔɨ | dʒʌst ɾísəntɨɨ | méni pɨ́φö
56 dón? ɫʌ́ɪk ɨʔ

There is a huge complex eh shopping centre / it's been all built up in the centre of the city / just recently. / Many people don't like it.

57 ən ɨʔ wəz ðɨ óɫd ë ʔístʌɾn skóʔɨʃ bʌ́s stéʃn̩ | ən̥ n̥ʌ́ʔ wəz
58 ó•ɫ ribɨ́ɫʔ

And it was the old Eastern Scottish bus station / and that was all rebuilt.

59 ɐ ɫɨ́v əbʌ́ʏʔ θɾí mʌɪɫz ʌ́ʏʔsʌɪd̥ ðə sɨ́ʔɨ an̥ ðə sʌ́ʏθ sʌɪd | an̥
60 ðə ɾód tə píbɫz pénɨk'ük' | ɨʔs ə | kʌ́ʏnsɫ hʌ́ʏzɨn ɨsté?

I live about three miles outside the city on the south side / on the road to Peebles, Penicuik. / It's a / council housing estate.

61 əpáɪʔ fəm ðə fʌ́ɪs θɾi mʌ́n̥θs

Apart from the first three months.

62 á•v bɨn gón fɾəm ðə tʌ́ʏn ðáʔ ɫɨ́n̥θ ə tʌ́ɪm

I've been gone from the town that length of time.

63 ɨnsáed̥ ðə sɨ́ʔɨ

Inside the city.

64 ɔɫ ðə ɾítɨ | ɛkskɫúzɨv hʌ́ʏzɨz | ðə ɾéts əɾ tú háɪ | fəɾ ə•
65 píp ɫ tə ɑ́ʔtʃəɫɨ ɫɨ́v̥ ðéɾ | so ðeɾ nʌ́ʍ tʌ́mɨn ɨntə ófɨsɨ̥z |

86

66   ɬʊʔs əv bɪznɪsɨz tʃɑɪʔəd əkʌ́ýnʔənts | tɾávɬ bɪznɪsɨz

All the really / exclusive houses / the rates are too high / for er people to actually live there / so they're now turning into offices / lots of businesses, chartered accountants / travel businesses.

67   ɐ wʌ́ɾk ən d̥ë kʌ́ýnte bʌ́sɨz | ʔɨkwɨvətənʔ ə kʌ́ʊ̯nʔe bʌ́sɨz
68   hiəɪ | əz fɑ́ɪ əz gɑ́ɬəʃíɬz ə gɬásgo ən nɔɾθ əz fɑ́ɪ əz pɛɾθ |
69   ɐ wʌ́ɾk ɒ̈n̥ ðɛm | wɨð ðá·ʔ kʌ́mpne dʒüən ðəh | vekéʃn | ən a
70   kən dʒə́st dɪtékt θɾü gon | fɑ́ɪv mʌ́ɪɬz ʌ̯ʊʔsʌ́ɪd̥ d̥ə sɨʔɨ tʊ̊ᵉ ə
71   pɬés kɔ́ɬb mʌ́sɬbʌɾʌʰ | ðe ə ʔáksɛ̈nts ɪíɬe dɨ́fɾən?

I work on the county buses / equivalent of county buses here / as far as Galashiels or Glasgow and north as far as Perth. / I work on them / with that company during the / vacation / and I can just detect through going / five miles outside the city to a place called Musselburgh / the er accent's really different.

72   pɸɛn ɐ wəz jʌ́ŋ | ɐ müvd ʌ́ý̯ʔsʌ́ɪd̥ d̥ə sɨʔɨ | bʌ́ʔ mʌ sɨ́stəɾz |
73   ðeɾ ɔɬ ółdə ðən me | wént' tə skǘɬ ʍɛ́ɾ ɐ wəz bɔ́ᵊn | so
74   ɨnstéd əv gon të ðə ɬókɬ skǘɬ ʍɛ ðə nü hʌ́ý̯zɨn ɨstéʔ wɒz |
75   wi tɾávɬd ɨn ɛvɾɨ dé tə ðɨ́s skǘɬ | ʍɛɾ m̥ ðə ɾɛ́st əv me
76   fá·mɬe hed gɔ́n | mʌ bɾʌ́ðð ən ʌ́ɪ | ɸɛn ɐ léft pɾáɪməɾe skǘɬ
77   ɐ went tə | ʔskǘɬ kɔ́ɬd sɨn? á·nθənɨz | kwʌ́ɪʔ nɪə ðə dɔ́ks

When I was young / I moved outside the city / but my sisters / they're all older than me / went to school where I was born / so instead of going to the local school where the new housing estate was / we travelled in every day to this school / where um the rest of my family had gone / my brother and I. / When I left primary school I went to / school called St. Anthony's / quite near the docks.

78   ɨn θʌ́ɾd̥ʒ˞ ʝ̊iəɾ | wɛn á wəz ɨn me θʌ́:d ʝíɾ ðə skǘɬ tɾanzféɪd
79   fɾəm ðaʔ bɨ́ldɨŋ ɨn ɬíθ ə tʊ̊ᵊ ʌ bɾɨ́ɬjənʔ pɬés at dʌ́dɨŋstn̩ |
80   ɒ̈n d̥ə wé tə mʌ́sɬbʌɾʌʰ | əʔ ðə bɔ́ʔm· ɑ́ɾθəɾz síʔ áʔtʃəɬe ɨn
81   hólɨɾüd pɑ́k | nɔʔ fɑ́ɪ fɾəm hólɨɾüd pɑ́ɾk ovəɾ ðɨ ʌ́ðəɾ̥ sǽɪd

In third year / when I was in my third year, the school transferred from that building in Leith er to a brilliant place at Duddingston / on the way to Musselburgh / at the bottom of Arthur's Seat actually in Holyrood Park / not far from Holyrood Park, over the other side.

82 wi θɔ́ʔ wi wüd kɪ́p ɔn | sɔɾʔ ə | a don no sʌ́m sɔɾʔ ə hɪ́stəɾɨ
83 ə ðáʔ ném | nʌ́y̌ ðə sɨ́ʔɨz sʌ́ɑvb bæɪ tǘ kɔmpɾɨhénsɨv káθɨɨk
84 skǘɫz wʌ́n fəɾ | wę́st sǽɪd wʌ́n fəɾ ð ɪ́s sǽɪd

We thought we would keep on / sort of / I don't know, some
sort of history of that name. / Now the city's served by
two comprehensive Catholic schools, one for / west side,
one for the east side.

85 ðəɪ̯ɡ mó_ɪ pɾʊ́tɨstənt skǘɫz ɨn édɨnbʌɾʌ | ðə pɾʊ́dɨstənt skǘɫz
86 sim tə bi mó_ɾ ɫókɫæɪzd | séɪ̯ʔn dɨ́stɾɨks əv ðə sɨ́tɨ

There's more Protestant schools in Edinburgh / The Protestant schools seem to be more localized / certain districts
of the city.

87 slá·ŋg | há·ŋ əɾʌ́ynd n ə gɾʊ́p | ma fá·ðəɾ jüs s ówɨz bi |
88 i jüs tʼ ówɨz tę́ɫ me tə stʊ́p séɨŋ má· ɨnstɛd əv máɪ

Slang / hang around in a group / My father used to always
be / he used to always tell me to stop saying [ma·] instead
of [maɪ].

89 pɪ́pɫ ténd' tə | spɪ́k moɾ ɫáɪk ðá·ʔ | nǽɪs tə tók' tə·

People tend to / speak more like that / Nice to talk to.

90 mɔ́ə nɨnsæɪd ɨn édɨnbʌɾʌ jɛ· ðɛɫ ɾɨfë̇ɪ të ðá·ʔ

Morningside in Edinburgh, yes, they'll refer to that.

91 wɪ́ tɛnd mi n fɾɛ́nz ténd' tə ɾéçəynǽɪz ɨf sʌ́mbəde fɾʊ́m ʌ
92 pɾɪ́vɪəsɫe pɾáɪvɨʔ skǘɫ kʌ́mz tə ðə ðɨs sékəndəɾe módəɾn ɔɾ
93 kómpɾɨhénsɨv

We tend, me and friends tend to recognize if somebody from
a previously private school comes to the this secondary
modern or comprehensive.

94 ðɛɫ tɾáɪ ən ɾɨfʌ́ɪn ðeɾ stá·ŋ kəɫókwɪəɫɨzmz

They'll try and refine their slang colloquialisms.

95 ɨf jü gó fəɾ ən ɪ́nʔʌvjü fəɾ ə dʒɔ́·b | sʌ́m pɪ́ɸɫ ɐ nó

If you go for an interview for a job. / Some people I know.

(v) *Phonological discussion*
There are a number of characteristics of Edinburgh speech which are quite different from those of the other accents discussed in this book. The main ones are: few, if any, contrasts between short and long vowels; no clear [l]; use of /x/, with positional variants [ç] and [x], which occurs not only in words of Gaelic origin, e.g. *Drumsheugh*, but also in English words: both speakers have [ç] in *recognize*, even though lenition of intervocalic stops is not a feature of this accent (see below); few diphthongal articulations; consistent use of /h/; consistent use of /ʍ/, though H has [w] in *when* on one occasion (78), and the realizations [pɸ] (72) and [f̰] (76); rhoticity; no /ɤ/ element; a variety of vowel qualities in unstressed syllables. The distinction between /æɪ/ and /ʌɪ/, discussed by Wells (1982: 405-06), does not appear to be relevant to either speaker, at least with any consistency. G uses a diphthong in the region of [æɪ~aɪ], with one instance of [ɐɪ] in *outside* (5); H has both types of articulation but not exclusive to any particular context, e.g. [haɪ] (64), [ʌɪ] (76), [bæɪ] (83); [ʌÿʔsʌɪd̰] (59), [ɨnsaed̰] (63).

Another characteristic which marks off this accent from the others discussed in this book is that the major processes discussed in the Introduction apply to a far lesser extent in both speakers.

H uses [ʔ] intervocalically for /t/, whereas G does not; H also uses [ʔ] for /k/ before /t/.

(a) *Lenition*. There is little or no lenition of the type, stop → fricative, or voiceless → voiced; H has two examples of the former: [piɸö] *people* (55), [rɛçəɣnæɪz] *recognize* (91), and one example of the latter: [prɒdɨstənt̰] *Protestant* (55). The two sounds that are affected most by lenition are /l/ and /r/. G vocalizes or even deletes /l/ quite regularly, e.g. [ɔ̈ö] *all* (14), [skuö] *school* (2) and (11), [sku:z] *schools* (52) x 2, [odər] *older* (12). H, on the other hand, does not usually°do so, though we must note [piɸö] (55) and [ɔwɨz] *always* (87) and (88). In the latter case we are dealing with /l/+/w/, the most likely environment for vocalization, then deletion; c.f. G's [sku wë] *school we* (11).

/r/, on the other hand, is vocalized and deleted by both speakers in post-vocalic position. The flap, with its slight closure phase, undergoes lenition first to a frictionless continuant, then to a central vowel [ə], then it is deleted, sometimes with a slight effect on the preceding vowel, e.g.

G	H	
[mʌɪtʃənt] *merchant* (52)	——	frictionless continuant
[koət] *court* (3) [ʃɔət] *short* (42)	[sʌəvb] *served* (83) [bɔən] *born* (73)	(slight) central vowel
[bʌdz̥] *birds* (38)(41)	[pɑk] *park* (81)	deletion
[ʌðəwaɪz] *otherwise* (48)	[ə] *or* (68)	deletion in unstressed syllable
[pɔʃʌ] *posher* (11)	[ɨnʔʌvjü] *interview* (95)	deletion + slight change in vowel quality
[fʌːst] *first* (21) [ʃɔ·t] *short* (47)	[θʌːd] *third* (78)	deletion + lengthening of vowel.

We must note that some words occur both with and without any r-sound in the surface version, e.g. [bʌɪdz] (38), [θʌɾd͡ʒ] (78), as well as the instances given above. It is most likely to be deleted before other post-alveolars, after the opening vowels /ʌ ɔ ɑ/, and finally in unstressed syllables. H has an example of intervocalic deletion: [dʒüən] *during* (69). There are no examples of "intrusive" linking /r/. (For a discussion of /r/ in a number of Edinburgh children, see Romaine, 1978.)

(b) *Devoicing*. As in the previous locality, we find devoicing of voiced sounds, in particular fricatives and /r/, before voiced sounds, usually in word-final position, although G also devoices initial /ð/ after a devoiced final /ð/. E.g.

[wəz̥ wɪð̥ ðæt] *was with that* (2)

[mɛðər̥ wɪð̥ ðë] *whether with the* (8)

[ɑv̥ afɛkteʃn̩] *of affectation* (14)

[hʌÿz̥ɨz] *houses* (64)

[ɨɨv̥ ðer] *live there* (65)

[wɨð̥ ða·ʔ] *with that* (69).

Final devoicing before a pause also applies to vowels occasionally, e.g. [edɪnbɾʌh] (51), [mʌsɨbʌɾʌh] (71), (80), and /r/ is also affected in this way, e.g. [odər̥] (12), [ɹiəɾ̥] (78). Devoicing before voiceless sounds, as in RP and most other accents, applies to /r/, within the word, too, e.g. [wʌɾk] (26), (67) and (69), and initial devoicing of /r/ occurs after voiceless stops and fricatives, e.g. [fr̥əm] (13) and (62), [tr̥es] (14). In one instance we find final devoicing of a vowel before a voiceless sound: [mɑ·hkədɫɪ̥] (31).

(c) *Harmony*. As with lenition, there is less evidence of harmony in the speech of these two informants than is the case in other accents. The place harmony of the alveolars displayed by most accents (cf. Introduction, and Lodge, 1981) is much more restricted in that it occurs most before the dentals and rarely elsewhere, except in the case of /n/ + velar (see below). For example:

[bət̪ ðəz̥] *but there's* (9)

[ət̪ ðə] *at the* (35)

[ʌÿʔsʌɪd̪ ðə] *outside the* (59)

[ɑn̪ ðə] *on the* (59)

[mʌn̪θs] *months* (61),

but [wʌn gɛts] (12), [ðən me] (73). G has one example of /s/-harmony, giving [koɾθ ðə] *course the* (14), but he has no harmonizing to bilabial or velar articulations. H has a few examples, but they are sporadic rather than regular:

[kɔɫb mʌsɫbʌɾʌʰ] *called Musselburgh* (71)

[sʌəvb bæɪ] *served by* (83).

In one case he has a double articulation: [θʌɾd͡ʒ͡ ʝiəɾ] (78), alongside non-harmonized [θʌːd ʝiə] (78). The one regular harmony of a post-alveolar to velarity is that of /n/ before /k/ and /g/ within the word, e.g. [θɪŋk] (48), [ɪŋgɫənd] (22), but we must note that it does not harmonize to bilabiality under the same conditions, as can be seen from both speakers' pronunciation of *Edinburgh*.

Manner harmony is restricted to /ð/-harmony, which is more common in H than in G, e.g.

[ən̪ næt̪ʔ] *on that* (23)

[tɛks səm] *takes them* (47) + voice harmony

[ɫn̪ n̪ə] *in the* (55)

[ən̪ d̪ë] *on the* (67),

alongside the non-harmonized forms, one of which, *on the* (59), is given above. There are no instances of

91

/ð/-harmony to /l/. H has two further instances of manner harmony, which are probably slips of the tongue rather than evidence of a phonological process, because of their unusual nature: [bɾʌðð] (76), [jüs s] (87).

Palatal harmony is more in evidence than the other types, though again there are occasions where it does not take place:

[aktʃetë] *actually* (5)

[ɛdʒükeʃn̩] *education* (9)

[ʌnjüʒɨ̩] *unusual* (43)

[aʔtʃətɨ] *actually* (65) and (80, with different final vowel)

[dʒüən̩] *during* (69),

but [ɨntɾədjüst] *introduced* (22)

[wəz jʌŋ] *was young* (72).

In one instance H has harmony between /l/ and a vowel: [ɨiθ] (79), where the vowel is retracted under the influence of the /l/-articulation.

(d) *CCS*. There are no examples of this in G's speech, but some in H's involving /t/ and /d/:

[fʌɪs θɾi] *first three* (61)

[is sæɪd] *east side* (84)

[dɨstɾɨks] *districts* (86)

[fɾɛnz̥] *friends* (91).

There is one example of /t/-deletion after /n/: [don no] (82), but there is insufficient evidence for us to decide whether /-nt/ behaves differently from any other /-Ct/ or not (cf. the other localities above).

There is a /g/-deletion rule to produce morpheme-final [ŋ], and H has the alternative [-ɨn] ending for words ending in unstressed *-ing*, whereas G has not.

(e) *UVD*. Once again, this process is not as widely applied as in other accents. Within the word unstressed syllables are sometimes deleted, sometimes retained, e.g. G's [kʌmpənɪ] (52) versus H's [kʌmpne] (69). This is not a pattern distinguishing the two speakers, because we also have G's [nobdë] (17) versus H's [sɛkəndəɾe] (92). The first of two contiguous unstressed vowels is sometimes deleted:

[bɔʔm· aɾ̩θəɾz̥] *bottom of Arthur's* (80)

[ð is] *the east* (84).

G has one example of reduction to a glide rather than deletion in [ðj ɐdmɪnɪstɹeʃn̩] (29-30).

(f) *Vowel lengthening.* /a/ is often lengthened, both where RP has /ɑ/ and elsewhere, especially before nasals, e.g.

[ɬaːft] *laughed* (3)
[haːmɬët] *hamlet* (6)
[səbstaːnʃəö] *substantial* (10)
[ðaːt aːksɛnt] *that accent* (10)
[ɹaːpɨdɬeʰ] *rapidly* (16)
[baːd] *bad* (16)
[aːfɹɨkən] *African* (40)
[a·v] *I've* (62)
[ða·ʔ] *that* (69), (89) and (90)
[fa·mɬe] *family* (76)
[a·nθənɨz̥] *Anthony's* (77)
[ha·ŋ] *hang* (87)
[fa·ðəɾ] *father* (87).

In the case of speaker H the vowel phase is usually shorter than that of G. These are not just the environments involved in Aitken's Law (see Aitken, 1962; Ewen, 1977; and Wells, 1982: 405-06), though these, too, produce lengthening on occasion, e.g.

[fjüː] *few* (16)
[fɑ·ɾ] *for* (17)
[kɔnfɛ·ɹ] *confer* (32).

Some of the instances of lengthening may be the effect of stress in lento speech, e.g. [ɬɔ·ts] (40) beside [ɬat] (22), [ɔ·d] (44), [dʒɔ·b] (95). In G's speech /e/ where it is equivalent to RP /e/ seems to be lengthened quite often, under a variety of circumstances, e.g.

[ɬe·s] *less* (31)
[wike·nd] *week-end* (35)
[e·g] *egg* (40)
[ənle·s] *unless* (47).

Lastly, loss of /r/ also produces lengthening of the

preceding vowel phase, e.g.

    [fʌːst] *first* (21)
    [mɑ·hkədɫɪ] *markedly* (31)
    [mɑ·kt] *marked* (53)
    [θʌːd] *third* (78).

Chapter Five

COVENTRY

There is one male informant, A, aged 68. He was born and educated in Coventry, but moved to Kenilworth at the age of 12.

(i) *General*
This speaker has an articulatory setting which in some respects resembles that of Liverpool speakers (cf. Knowles, 1978: 89). The pharynx walls are tightened and the faucal opening is quite narrow: there is an adenoidal quality to much of his speech (cf. Knowles, ibid.). The synchronization of velic closure throughout the continuum does not always take account of phonological segmentation. Consequently, whole stretches of speech may be slightly, or even heavily nasalized; on the other hand, nasal segments are sometimes only nasal for half their duration, and occasionally not nasal at all. The half-nasality I have indicated by means of the appropriate non-nasal letter with a tilde, e.g. [ã].

/t d s z n/ are all post-alveolar, and the fricative pair are not grooved, making them sound very like /ʃ ʒ/. /t d n/ are usually dental before /ð/. /l/ is always velarized.

The voiceless stops are rarely aspirated, but are often slightly affricated, especially /t/.

Lip-rounding is produced by parting at the centre only (cf. Stockport, above). It is widespread, associated not only with the "rounded" vowels, but with consonants and unstressed vowels too.

(ii) *Vowel diagrams*

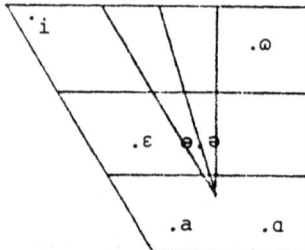

short monophthongs

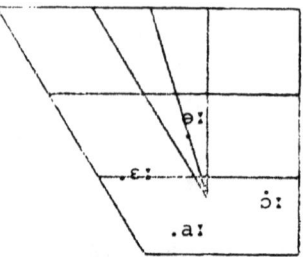

long monophthongs

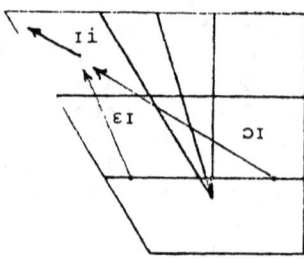

front closing
diphthongs

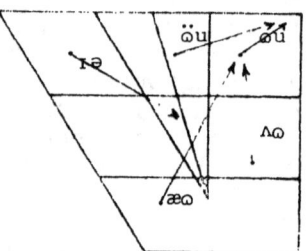

back closing
diphthongs
and [ɪə]

(iii) *The transcription*

1 jɛ ɔɪ júus tʻav ə kʌ́ɔ̃zən | wɛn iʔ wəz̥ féːst ʌ̃ɔpm̩ ʃɪi wəz ɪn̥
2 n̥ə káʃbɑks

Yes, I used to have a cousin / when it was first open, she was in the cashbox.

3 gíi jəɾ ɛ́niθiŋ̃ tʃɾ́ip

Give you anything cheap.

4 blʌ́ɔkʔ kʊm ɹǽɔnd' | ʃʌ́vd ə káːd θɹɔu ðə dɔ́ː

Bloke come round / shoved a card through the door.

5 bɒd̥ ðə wəz̥ sʌ́mbdi ɛ́ɫs kʊm ð ʌ́ðə dɛɪ ə wʌ́mən

But there was somebody else come the other day, a woman.

6 ʃi kʌ́m wɔːɫ ɔ́ː wɔ́ːn̩ʔ n̩ɛ́ː

She come while I wasn't there.

7 äɫ ɫəz ə fáːm ʏp ɑn̥ n̥ə ɹɔ́ɪtʻ fɹəm m̃n̩ɛ́ː | bifɔ́ː ðə bɔ́ɪpas |
8 ən ɔɪ síi ðis | kǽɔdɔŋ | dʒɔst ʌ́ɔvə ðə fɛ́ns | ən äd gád ə |
9 lɪtɫ sánbag wi mi | ɔ̈ pʌ́d itʻ íṯ̚ dis sámbag wi gáɹ äm bʻ bɔz̥

Well, there's a farm up on the right from there / Before the by-pass / And I see this / cow dung / just over the fence / and I'd got a / little sand-bag with me. / I put it in this sand-bag, we got on the bus.

10 nä́ʔ ɫaːst ɾístə ʃɔ́ːɫi

Not last Easter, surely?

11 ʃi wɒn áːf

She won't half.

12 iz zä́ʔ ʔə tʻɛ́ɫifʌɔm báks | nɛks dɔ́ː

Is that the telephone box / next door?

13 iʔ wəz nɛ́ks dɔ́ː tə ðä́ʔ wɛɹ áɫis wəz tɛ́kin ə fʌ́ɔtʏ· insɔ́ɪd̥
14 ðatʻ

It was next door to that, where Alice was taking a photo inside that.

15 ɔɪ stɨ́ɫ wéːɾ iʔ næ̃ω | naʔs əβaω? | éɪtɪin íəɪ əgωu
I still wear it now / and that's about eighteen year ago.

16 äɛv ad ə bɫóu ən | ðə séɪm sɔ́ːt
I've had a blue one / the same sort.

17 djə ɹékən nəz̥ tóu
Do you reckon there's two?

18 ən ɪi sɛ́z ɔ́ɪ wəz zə bɫɅ́ok əz əd: tóg id ǽᴜt | tóu fɔ́t əv
19 ém mənɔ́uəɹ iṇ ṇatˀ tắp fɫắtˀ
And he says, I was the bloke as had took it out / two foot of hen manure in that top flat.

20 iz dʒɔ́ɪs stiɫ ɫé·
Is Joyce still there?

21 méni æωɹ ətˀ dắtˀ | fɔ́ɪvstɅωː wɛn ɔ́ wəz ə kíd
Many hour at that / fivestones, when I was a kid.

22 dídntʃə tɛk nɅω fɅ́otɅωz əv ðắtˀ
Didn't you take no photos of that?

23 iz zắʔ ʔə séɪm wán
Is that the same one?

24 ä bɔ́ːt ɹ ə plánt əž ʃi tɅ́oɫ mi ði ɔ́ðə wɹ́ik i cɫɅ́oziz inː
25 nɔ́ɪt ən kωmz ǽωt iṇ ṇə déɪtɔɪm
I bought her a plant and she told me the other week, it closes in the night and comes out in the day-time.

26 ä́ dɅωmʔ báɾə tə ɹimémbə néɪmz̥
I don't bother to remember names.

27 ä bɔ́ːt ə θɹíi | in ə pát | ən ʃi tóg̊ ə ɫíif ɔːf ðát
I bought her three / in a pot / and she took a leaf off that.

28 éːd ə ðə wíndə | ðɛɾ ɔ́ː ɹɔ́ɪpʰ bɒt | ɔ̈ ɬɔ́ːst ə ɬát əv əm
    Out of the window / They're all right but / I lost a lot of them.

29 äbʰ pɔ́ɹ ə ɬaɾ ə kɔ́tinz ínː pɑ́ts bɒt̪ʰ d̪ɛɪː kɔ́m tə nɔ̈́θiŋg̊
    I'd put a lot of cuttings in pots but they come to nothing.

30 jɵu kán kíɬ əm
    You can kill them.

31 ä bɛ́ɾ iz ʒəɹɛ́ɪnjəmz əɹ | gɛ́ɾin ɹɛ́di næ̃ɵ nɪ́əli fə | pɬántin
32 æ̃ɒt | ɪiɬ av fɬæ̃ɵez ɑˑn əm bifɔ́ːɾ ɪi pɑ́ts əm æ̃ɒt | ɹid ad
33 ɬáːʃ ɪə
    I bet his geraniums are / getting ready now nearly for / planting out. / He'll have flowers on them before he puts them out / He'd had last year.

34 sɵm píŋkiɹ wɔ́nz | bɒt íz n jɵu síi iz gáːdin | in ðə
35 sɔ́mətɔɹm ən iz wán píktʃə | ɪi gɹʌ́ɵz bígis páːt ɒn it
36 izsɛ́öf
    Some pinky ones / but his ... and you see his garden / in the summertime and it's one picture / He grows biggest part on it hisself.

37 ɛ́ː dʒɑnz gáːdin it stɹɛ́tʃiz fɹəm | fɹəm íə tiˑ ðə bákʰ gɛ́ɪt
    Our John's garden it stretches from / from here to the back gate.

38 ʃɹi dídn̩ kɵm íw̃ wán dɛɪ
    She didn't come in one day.

39 əɹ ʌ́zbən jɔ́ustʰ bi ɑn̩ n̪ə kəmíti ɵp ðə cɬʌ́b jɹəz ən jɹəz əgɔ́u
    Her husband used to be on the committee up the club years and years ago.

40 ðəz tɔ́u síɬinz ä wán im tə dɔ́u wán in̩ n̪ə fɹʌ́n? bɛ́dɹɵum əw̃
41 wan in̩ n̪ə | mídɬ ɹɵum dæ̃ɒnstɛ́ːz
    There's two ceilings I want him to do, one in the front bedroom and one in the / middle room downstairs.

99

42 ä wén ɛ:ˀ n̩ fɹɔ́ɪdɪi | ən á:θəz béː:θdɛɪ
    I went out on Friday / on Arthur's birthday.

43 ɪi ɛ́ĩˀ bin dæɒn wið ə | bɒɾ ɪiz véɾi veɾi kwɔ́ɾət
    He ain't been down with her / but he's very, very quiet.

44 əz ʌɷni θɹíi ä̃m əm
    There's only three on them.

45 jɷβ sín dʒánz ɛ́ĩˀ jə | wɛɬ jɷ sin wán əv əm
    You've seen John's, ain't you? / Well, you seen one of them.

46 wɛɬ ɔ́:ɬ áv it̚ˀ | a gaɾ ə fɔ́ɪn sɔ́mmɒ̃ni næɷ tə kɒm ən töun it |
47 i wants töunin | i sɛ d̪iˀ pjánə ɾɷnə á:f wɑnˀ töunin
    Well, I'll have it. / I got to find somebody now to come and
    tune it / it wants tuning / He said, This piano doesn't half
    want tuning.

48 ä ʃá:mˀ báðə
    I shan't bother.

49 tʃápiw̃ wód ən: ðáˀ | ən̪ n̪ém wɛn ɔ́ lɛ́f skɷɬ ɔ́ wɛn̪ˀ n̪e:
50 pé:mənənt
    Chopping wood and that / and then when I left school I went
    there permanent.

51 ən ä wén in̪ n̪i áfis | ən ä jɷsᵗ sə gɔ́u wi ði ɔ́:siz | ɔ́ jɷs
52 də ɹɔ́ɪd̪ də tʃɛ́ɪnɔ:s
    And I went into the office / and I used to go with the
    horses / I used to ride the chain-horse.

53 ðə fɹɷ̃́w̃ˀ w̃ɒ̃n
    The front one.

54 ə big fɔ́ɪə dæɒn̪ n̪ɛ́: á:ʰtə wi wə máɪid n̪ its ɔ́:ɬ gɑt̚ bəːnt
55 æ̃ɒt
    A big fire down there after we were married and it's all
    got burnt out.

56 sɛptémbə twɛði fɔ́ɪv | i wə bɔːt ǿp wið əm | dʒɔ́ːdʒ bɔːt ím
57 ǿp
   September '25 / He were brought up with m / George brought him up.

58 mi áːnti ad ʔǽɒs | ðɛ́ː ən̩ ðə dɹɔ́ɪv wɛnd ǿp íə
   My auntie had a house / there, and the drive went up here.

59 əkɹɔ́ːs zə ɹʌ̊ɒψ fɹəm ðɛ́m | wɛɫ ɛɪ wə bʌ̊ɒθ əkɹɔ́ːs zə ɹʌ̊ɒd
   Across the road from them / Well, they were both across the road.

60 mi dǽd wəz iŋ n̩ə tə́im
   My dad was in the team.

61 ðə wík˺ bifɔ́ː wid˺ bin pɫɛ́ɪiŋ n̩ə ɫíidʒən
   The week before we'd been playing the Legion.

62 if jǿ k̩ bïit ím | wi kũ wín n̩ís
   If you can beat him / we can win this.

63 ɔɪ θíŋ̊ ik˺ kɔ́ːs mi tɛ́n pǽɒnd
   I think it cost me ten pound.

64 ðə jǿus tə bɹi ə ʃáft | ɹɒ́niŋ θɹʊ́u | ði ǽɒziz̥
   There used to be a shaft / running through the houses.

65 f ä̃ɪŋ gǿnə stǽp mb fɔ̃ɪm mĩ wɛɪ nǽɒ ɔɪ θĩŋk ɔɪ ʃɒb˺ bi ɫǽss |
66 ɔ́ː ɫə ɹɛ́st wə dʒǿst | stɹɛ́ɪt ǽɒt ǽntə ðə pǽθ
   If I'm going to stop and find my way now, I think I should be lost / All the rest were just / straight out onto the path.

67 ðə wz ʌ̃ɒni mɹi ðíə də ɫɒ̊k áːtə mi mǿðə
   There was only me there to look after my mother.

68 bɒʔ də sɛ́ɪm pɫ́ɪpɫ̩ kɛ́p it | əz kɛ́p it | wɛ̃ mǿðə wəz ə kíd
   But the same people kept it / as kept it / when mother was a kid.

69 káptin áːst im də gə d∉ɒn̩ ðə ɫɔ́ɪw̃ wɔ́ns

   Captain asked him to go down the line once.

70 ðə báːθɹɒum wəz zə fə́s dʒɑb

   The bathroom was the first job.

(iv) *Phonological discussion*
This accent can be seen as sharing some characteristics with more northerly ones and some with southern ones (cf. Wells, 1982: 363); thus, there is no /ɒ/-/ʌ/ distinction, but words with the diphthong of *time* have a realization [ɔɪ] (and there may be no distinction between *buy* and *boy*, cf. Wells, ibid.). Also there is fluctuation between [a] and [aː], [ɑ] and [ɔː] before voiceless fricatives (see below). /h/ does not occur, nor does syllable-final /r/. There is inconsistent use of final [ŋ] and [ŋg̊] (see below).

   The definite article is often omitted as a result of a number of processes, as exemplified below; there is no evidence of the glottal stop realization, as found in Stockport (see Chapter 1).

(a) *Lenition*. The most common lenition applies to voiceless stops, which are either realized as lenes or completely voiced, usually in intervocalic position, but also elsewhere, e.g.

   [bɒd̥ ðə] *but the* (5)

   [tɒg̊ ə] *took a* (27)

   [jɒs d̥ə] *used to* (51-52)

   [θiŋg̊] *think* (63)

   [gɑd ə] *got a* (8)

   [tɒg id æɒt] *took it out* (18)

   [ɛːd ə] *out of* (28)

   [wɛnd ɒp] *went up* (58).

Flaps are sometimes used, e.g. [gɛɾin] *getting* (31), [pjanə ɾɒnə] *piano doesn't* (47), and lenition to a frictionless contunuant also takes place, e.g. [gɑɹ äm] *got on* (9). Occasionally, lenition from stop to fricative takes place, e.g. [əβaʊʔ] *about* (15). Vocalization and deletion of /l/ are not common, e.g.

   [ɔː ɹɔɪp̚] *all right* (28)

   [izsɛöf] *hisself* (36).

(b) *Harmony*. As in the other accents, the commonest sounds which undergo place harmony are the alveolars, e.g.

[bo̞d̪ ðə] *but the* (5)

[äm bˀ bo̞z̪] *on the bus* (9)

[ɛm mənɷuəɹ] *hen manure* (19)

[n̪ɛm wɛn] *then when* (49)

[ɹʌɷʮ fɹəm] *road from* (59).

There are exceptions and variation, e.g.

[tɛn pæo̞nd] *ten pound* (63)

[ən ko̞mz] *and comes* (25)

[didn̩ ko̞m] *didn't come* (38)

[fɹɷn? bɛd-] *front bed-* (40)

and [sanbag] alongside [sambag] *sandbag* (9). [äm əm] *on them* (44) is an example of non-contiguous harmony which seems to be exceptional. There is one example of /m/ harmonizing its place of articulation: [äĩŋ gənə] *I'm going to* (65). In the case of [stɑp mb fɔ̃ĩm] *stop and find* (65) the syllabic masal and' following stop harmonize with the preceding consonant, not the following one.

Palatization of /t d s z/ also occurs:

[didn̩tʃə] *didn't you* (22)

[iʒ ʒəɹɛɪnjəmz] *his geraniums* (31)

[ɬaːʃ ɪə] *last year* (33),

though there is one instance where it does not apply: [djə] (17).

/ð/ harmonizes as to manner, even to an oral stop after a stop, e.g.

[in̪ n̪ə] *in the* (1-2)

[wɔːn̪? n̪ɛ] *wasn't there* (6)

[äɬ ɬəz] *well, there's* (7)

[fɹəm m͡n̪ɛ̃ː] *from there* (7)

[it̪ˀ d̪is] *in this* (9)

[äm bˀ bo̞z̪] *on the bus* (9)

[iz za? ?ə] *is that the* (12) and (23)

[ət̪ˀ d̪at] *at that* (21)

[bo̞? d̪ə] *but the* (68).

In [sɛ d̪i ʔ] *said this* (47) Geminate Simplification has been applied. In one instance we have an alveolar nasal (and no unstressed vowel) for the definite article: [in: nɔɪt] (24-25), and in another case a flap articulation is used: [baɾə] *bother* (26). There is also one instance of devoicing following /s/: [əkɹɔ:s zə] (59).

Manner harmony, with place harmony as appropriate, also applies to the alveolars, e.g.

[iw̃ wɑn] *in one* (38)

[fɹõw̃ʔ w̃õn] *front one* (53)

[kũ wiṇ̊] *can win* (62).

In [əž ʃi] *and she* (24), palatal harmony has not taken place. /t/ harmonizes to a fricative after /s/ occasionally:

[jʊsᵗ sə] *used to* (51)

[ɫɑss] *lost* (65).

In [fɔɪvstʌɵw̃: wɛn] *fivestones when* (21) both /n/ and /z/ harmonize with the following /w/.

Nasalization and denasalization have already been mentioned above as a general phonetic feature of this speaker. In some instances nasality occurs as a consequence of the deletion of the stop feature of /n/, as in the case of other accents, e.g. [ɛĩʔ] *ain't* (43) and (45), but there are also instances where nasality occurs over a considerable number of segments, e.g.

[sɒmmõni] *somebody* (46)

[fɹõw̃ʔ w̃õn] *front one* (53)

[fõĩm mĩ] *find me* (65).

(c) *CCS*. This applies to /t/ and /d/, as in the other accents, in morpheme-final position followed by another consonant, e.g.

[nɛks dɔ:] *next door* (12)

[tʌʊɫ mi] *told me* (24)

[bigis pa:t] *biggest part* (35)

[fõĩm mĩ] *find me* (65).

/k/, too, is deleted in the context /s/___C, e.g. [a:st] *asked* (60). In one instance the /d/ of initial /dʒ/ is deleted: [iʒ ʒəɪɛɪnjəmz] (31), but this may be exceptional.

The modified version of Geminate Simplification, discussed above in Peasmarsh, in which two matched

place features trigger the deletion of the second
segment containing the matched feature (which would
seem to have to be alveolar), appears to operate in
A's speech, as in:

[wɒn] *wouldn't* (11)

[didn̩] *didn't* (38)

[ɒzbən] *husband* (39)

[wɑn] *want* (40)

[wɛn] *went* (42) and (51).

That this is not CCS operating is demonstrated by the
fact that, with the exception of the examples at (38)
and (39), a vowel follows. There is one instance
where the final /t/ is not deleted but voiced: [wɛnd
ɒp] *went up* (58). There are no examples of left-to-
right Nasal Harmony, resulting in [nn], as in Shepherd's Bush and Peasmarsh.

In other instances Geminate Simplification
applies as in the other accents, e.g.

[ɔː ɬə] *all the* (66)

[wɛ̃ mɒðə] *when mother* (68).

Final [ŋ] occurs without a following [g], but
also with both nasal and oral stop articulations,
even before a pause: compare [-dɑŋ] (8) with [nɒθiŋg̊]
(29). /g/-deletion also applies, as in [töunin] (49),
[tʃɑpiw̃ wɒd] (49), with Manner Harmony as well in the
latter example.

(d) *UVD*. Unstressed vowels are deleted when two
vowels come together across word-boundaries, e.g.

[t av] *to have* (1)

[ð ɒðə] *the other* (5).

Often, when the stress pattern is V́C$_n$V̆C$_n$V̆, where C$_n$
may be one or more consonants, the middle vowel is
deleted, as in:

[sɔ́mbdi] *somebody* (5)

[bɔ́ːt ɪ ə] *bought her a* (24)

[jǿustʔ bi] *used to be* (39).

Even with other stress patterns, deletion occurs,
e.g.

[inː nɔ́ɪt] *in the night* (24-25)

[ad ʔǽɒs] *had a house* (58)

105

[ðə wz ʌɔni] *there was only* (67).

Utterance-initial unstressed vowels disappear occasionally, as in: [f ä̃ĩŋ] *If I'm* (65).

(e) *Vowel lengthening*. Before voiceless fricatives there is fluctuation in the application of lengthening, even in the same word, e.g.

    [ɔːf] (27)   [ʃaft] (64);

    [ɫɔːst] (28)   [ɫass] (65);

    [baːθ-] (70)   [paθ] (66).

Before /-nC/ there seems to be no lengthening: [pɫantin] (31).

(f) *Linking r*. Linking r is used, sometimes as a flap, even when there is no underlying /r/; sometimes it does not occur, though, e.g.

    [jəɾ ɛniθiɡ̃] *you anything* (3)

    [ɪəɹ əgɔu] *year ago* (15)

    [ɾʌnə aːf] *doesn't half* (47).

(g) *Derivations*. To demonstrate the interaction of the processes, I give three sample derivations below, two of which show how the definite article is reduced and deleted:

                          /an ðɪi bɔz/

Stress placement   ⇒   än ðə bɔ́z

UVD   ⇒   än ð bɔ́z

/ð/-harmony   ⇒   än b bɔ́z

Place harmony   ⇒   [äm b bɔ́z̥] (9).

                         /wɛn mɔðr̩ + C/

Stress placement   ⇒   wɛn mɔ́ðr̩ C-

/r/-realization   ⇒   wɛn mɔ́ðə C-

Nasalization   ⇒   wɛ̃n mɔ́ðə

Place harmony   ⇒   wɛ̃m mɔ́ðə

Geminate simplif. ⇒   [wɛ̃ mɔ́ðə] (68).

                    /gɹʌɔz ðɪi bigist/
      Stress placement   =   gɹʌ́ɔz ðə bígist
      / ð/-harmony   =   gɹʌ́ɔz zə bígist
      Geminate Simplif.   =   gɹʌ́ɔz ə bígist
      UVD   =   [gɹʌ́ɔz bígis] (35),
where CCS removes the final /t/ of *biggest*.

Chapter Six

NORWICH

There is one informant, E, male, aged 68. He was born in Norwich and has lived there all his life.

(i) *General*
For a detailed description of the articulatory setting of many Norwich speakers, see Trudgill (1974: 185-91). E has a relatively tense musculature, occasional stretches of creaky voice, particularly in the neighbourhood of glottal stops, and sometimes his low, front vowels are nasalized slightly.

The voiceless stops are usually, but not always aspirated in syllable-initial position, and /t/ is often affricated as well. /l/ takes on the quality of the following vowel in word-initial position, so that, for example, [lɛf] *left*, [lɨʔɨ] *little* and [ɫɔk] *look* all have slightly different qualities in the first sound.

Lip-rounding is not particularly marked except in /ɔː/. It is associated with the bilabial sounds, giving a slight rounded quality to a following back vowel, as indicated in the transcription, and /aɪ/ after other sounds too, such as /l/ and /r/, is sometimes realized as [ɒɪ].

Glottal reinforcement of the voiceless stops is used, even in intervocalic position. The synchronization of the two closures varies to some extent, but I have not indicated this below.

The amount of retraction of the tongue for /r/ varies, as indicated in the difference between [ɹ] and [ɻ]; in one instance a retroflex tap is used:[ɽ].

The rhythm of Norwich speech is unlike that of the other accents discussed in this book. The quantity of both stressed and unstressed vowels varies considerably, and length of both monophthongs and diphthongs in stressed syllables may be considerable (cf. Wells, 1982: 341).

(ii) *Vowel diagrams*

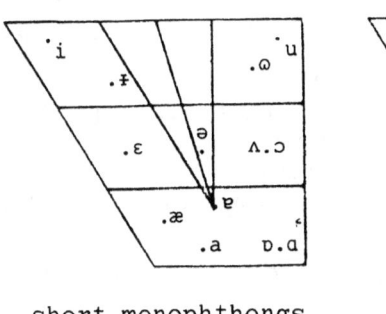

short monophthongs

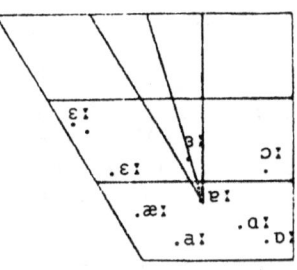

long monophthongs

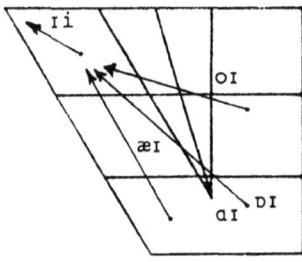

front closing
diphthongs

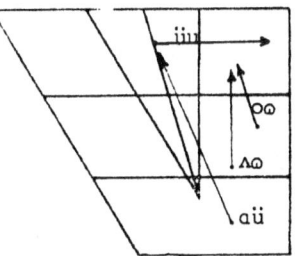

back closing
diphthongs and [aü]

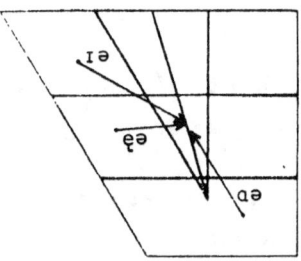

centring diphthongs

(iii) *The transcription*

1 ɨf áɪ wentˀ t'ə ðə lɨ̠ˀɫ vɨ̠lɨdʒəz áü?saɪd ná:ɪɨdʒ | dɹǽɪˀn
2 t'ǽɪvɹəm ɛ́nɨwɛ: ɫaɪ? ðǽ:? | aɪ æd əbáü? ə θɹíi maɪɫ kʌ́nˀɹi
3 wɔ́:kˀ tə gétˀ tɜ:m | ən wɔ́ns aɪ gá:? ðɛ: | ðɛɪ núu aɪ wəz ə
4 sɨ̠ˀi kɨd əz sunz ɛ́vɹ aɪ óꭢpmz mə máüθ

If I went to the little villages outside Norwich / Drayton,
Taverham, anywhere like that / I had about a three-mile
country walk to get to them / And once I got there / they
knew I was a city kid as soon as ever I opens my mouth.

5 ðə dɨ́fˀəns twɨn̪ ðə ná:ɪɨdʒ dáələkt ən̪ n̪ə nɔ́:fəkˀ dáələkt wəz
6 t'əɹɨ́fɨk

The difference between the Norwich dialect and the Norfolk
dialect was terrific.

7 ðæɪ wɛnˀ ɨ́nˀəɪ ə ʃá:pˀ tə bóɪ sʌ́fɨŋ

They went into a shop to buy something.

8 ðæɪ wəɪ ǽ:pɨ

They were happy.

9 aɪ gá:? ʌ́p ə lɨ̠ˀɫ bɨ? ʃá:pɨʃ ən aɪ k'ɔ́:? maɪ éd a·n ə bɨ? ə
10 p'óɪp

I got up a little bit sharpish and I caught my head on a bit
of pipe.

11 wɛ̈ ɫə blók nɛ́ks tüu mɨ wəz ə sɨ̠ˀi blok

Well, the bloke next to me was a city bloke.

12 ðæɪg gɨ́v əm ə pɒ́k ə ðə ɫʌ́g əz sunz zæɪd ɫɒ́k ǽ:ˀ ə̃m

They'd give them a poke at the lug as soon as they'd look at them.

13 ða? wəz ðə ɹʌ́fəs p'ɫɛ́:s ðɛ: wɔ́z

That was the roughest place there was.

14 ən̪ n̪ə bɹ́im wɒˀ wɛnˀ əkɹɔ́:st ad ðə jóoɫᵈz dɹɨ́ɫd ɨn əˀ wɛ: ði
15 oꭢɫ ɫɔ́:m jüus tə fɨ́ks

And the beam what went across had the holes drilled in it
where the old loom used to fix.

110

16 ðæɪ ɔ́ːɫwɪst ǽd ən ɪnvéː^ʔəd ɔ́ːʃüu ǽːŋɪn oʘvə ðə fɹʌ́nʔ dɔ́ː fə
17 lʌ́·k

They always had an inverted horse-shoe hanging over the front door for luck.

18 tʃʌ́x ə^ʔ oʘvə jə léf ʃʌ̰ɫdə | ən wɔ́ːkˀ kwʊɪə^ʔli əwǽɪ wɪðaü^ʔ
19 ɫʊ́kt̪ bɪʊ́ɪnd

Chuck it over your left shoulder / and walk quietly away without looking behind.

20 mʊ́ɪnd ʒüu | ɪf jüu ɜːdˀ gɫáːs əbɹɛ́ːkən áːftə jüudˀ tʃʌ́kt̪ ðæʔ
21 óʘvə jɔː ʃʌ̰ɫdə | jüudˀ pʊ́ɾ əʔ θɹüu sʌ́mwʌn^dz wɪ́ndə

Mind you / if you heard glass a-breaking after you'd chucked that over your shoulder / you'd put it through someone's window.

22 wén̪ ɲi ʌ̰ɫ dévəɫ ɫʊ́kˀ daüṋ ṋə tʃɪ́mnɪ | ən sɔ́ː ðæʔ pɔ́ɪnʔ ə
23 ðǽːʔ p'ʊ́kə p'ʊ́kən ʌ́p ǽːʔ ə̃m̃ | íɪbˀ bi aüʔ ðæʔ tʃɪ́mlɪ̄ p'áːʔ
24 ɫʊɪkˀ gɹíɪz ɫʊ́ɪʔnən | ǽːṋd ði ʌ̰ɫ fáː ɪ əd stáːʔ dɹɔ́ːɹən

When the old devil looked down the chimney / and saw that point of that poker poking up at him / he'd be out of that chimney pot like grease lightning / And the old fire would start drawing.

25 ən ɫʊ́ktˀ áːʔəɪ̱ əʔ | nóʘbʊ·di ɪn ði áüs əd évə wɔ́ːnʔ

And looked after it / nobody in the house would ever want.

26 fɹəm ɛ́ː ʔɪ | maüsʌ̰ɫd ən̪ ṋaʔ wón̪ʔ ə bɹɔ́ːk

From here to / Mousehold and that wouldn't have broke.

27 jü dɪn̪ʔ æv t'áɪŋ fə nóʘ bɹɛ́ːkfəst | ən aʒ jü wɔ́ːkt əɫáːŋ ðɛ̈
28 wəʒ jǘʒəɫi ə k'ʌ̰ɫ nɪ́p ɪṋ ɲi ɛ́ː | əm bə ðə t'áɪm jü gáːt̪
29 ðɛ· jü wónʔ áːf ʌ́ːŋgɹɪ

You didn't have time for no breakfast / and as you walked along, there was usually a cold nip in the air / and by the time you got there, you weren't half hungry.

30 wʊnʃ jüudˀ tɛ́ːstɪd ɪz ɹʊ́s tɛ́ːʔəz | ðass sʌ́fən jüud ɹɪmémbə
31 fə ðə ɹést ə jə ɫʊ́ɪf | ðæɪ wə büuʔəfɫ

111

Once you'd tasted his roast taters / that's something you'd remember for the rest of your life / They were beautiful.

32 ən i nŭ əʔ ɔ́ːɫ ɔ́ːf bəɪ̄ ɑ́ːʔ
And he knew it all off by heart.

33 mɔ́st ə ði ʌʊɫ wŕivz əd' tén̰ʔ ʔə ʃúumḛ́ːkən
Most of the old weavers had turned to shoemaking.

34 ɪid sʌ́mtɪmz goʊ dáün ʔə wɔ́ːʔə lḛ́ːn stǽɪð ən t'ɔ́ːkʰ tə̇ɪ́ ɛ́nɪ
35 ði ʌʊɫ wɛ́ɪɪmən
He'd sometimes go down to Water Lane Staithe and talk to any of the old wherrymen.

36 p'ɪ́k ʌp stʌ́f ɔːf ðə fɑ́ːɪən bɔ́ts wɒʔ pʊʔ ɪ̇n̰ ðɛɪ́ ən bɪɪ́ŋ əʔ
37 ɔ́ːɫ bǽːkʰ dáün ʔə nɑ́ːɪɪdʒ̊
Pick up stuff off the foreign boats what put in there and bring it all back down to Norwich.

38 ɪi wəz go ʔə sḛ́ːv ʌp ɔ́ːɫ ɪz mɔ́nɪ
He was going to save up all his money.

39 ɑ́ːɪɪk'ɑ́ʔ bŕinz wɪð ə bɪ́ʔ ə bḛ́ːçən bɔ́ɪɫd ɪn wɪ́·ð əʔ | kos
40 sæɪ dɪ́ʔn ɪiʔ ðə bḛ́ːçən ðə sǽɪm dǽɪ | ðaʔ wz ʌʊnɪ fɫḛ́ːvəɪ̄ən
Haricot beans with a bit of bacon boiled in with it / Course they didn't eat the bacon the same day / That was only flavouring.

41 ɪi ǽtʰ t'ə goʊ dáün gʌ́ʊɫdən dɔːg lḛ́ːn | ðɛ̈́ wəz ən ʌʊɫd ɪ́ǖənd'
42 tʃɛ́tʃ ɑ́ːf wæɪ dáün | ɪi wz ʌʊni baǘʔ sɛ́vən əɪ̄ ǽɪʔ | ən ɪ
43 jüs tə ʔɑ́ːp əɫɑ́ːŋ
He had to go down Golden Dog Lane. / There was an old ruined church half way down / He was only about seven or eight / and he used to hop along.

44 ðɛ̈́ wəz wɔ́n stɔ́ṇ ŋɛ́ː | ə bɪ́ʔ bɪ́gɪ̄ ən ɔ́ːɫ ɫə ɪɛst
There was one stone there / a bit bigger than all the rest.

45 ʊɪ névəɪ̄ ɜ́ːḍ ðǽʔ wɛd əfɔ́ː | soʊ ʔɪi dɪ́dnʔ bɑ́ːðə ʔ ɑ́ːsk

I never heard that word afore / So he didn't bother to ask.

46 ðɛm ɫʌ́vɨɫ gʌ́ʌɫ lɛ́ʔəz | ɹɪ́ɪʔ əkɹɔ́:s ðə stɹɪ́ɪʔ
Them lovely gold letters / Right across the street.

47 fə sʌ́fṭ ʔ ɪ́i? | ʃɨ wəz ə ɹʌ́f ʌʌɫ gɛ́ɫ | ðæɪ ɛd̚ p'ɫɛ́ʔi ə
48 t'ɑ́ɪm
For something to eat / She was a rough old girl / They had plenty of time.

49 ʌ́ŋkɫ ɝ́:bəʔ ɔ́:ɫwəz gɑʔ ʔɑ́:n? ʔɑ́:ɹiəʔs kɹɨ́sməs pɹɛ́zənʔ ɔ:f ɝ́:
Uncle Herbert always got Aunt Harriet's Christmas present off her.

50 ɨ gɑʔ ɹɛ́:znz ən ɨ spɹɛ́d̚ ðɪiz ɹɛ́:znz ɔ́:ɫ oʊvə ðə t'ɨ́n tɹǽɪ
He got raisins and he spread these raisins all over the tin tray.

51 soʊ ɪi ɔ́:ɫəs sʌ́ŋ ə k'ʌ́nʔɹɨ sɑ́:ŋ
So he always sung a country song.

52 ɛ́vɹɨ t'ɑɪm ṇə k'ɛ́ʔənz k'ʌm dɑ́ʊn ðɛ́ wəz ṇnʌ́ðə p'ɨ́ktʃə jüus
53 tə k'ʌ́m əkɹɔ́:st̚
Every time the curtains come down, there was another picture used to come across.

54 mɑ́ʊnʔ vəsüuviəs ɨn əɹʌ́ptʃn | ɛ́nɨbɑ·dɨ xəd̚ góʊ ɨn ən wɔ́:tʃ
Mount Vesuvius in eruption / Anybody could go in and watch.

55 ʃɪi æd lɛ́gz zə sɛ́:m əz ɛ́nɨwɔn ɛ́ɫs zɑʔ wəz ɛ́: ɹəfɫɛ́kʃən ɨn
56 ðə k'ǽ:bnəʔ
She had legs the same as anyone else, that was her reflection in the cabinet.

57 ɨ jüsʔ ə goʊ dǘʔ tə fǽɫθɔ:p wódz | gǽðəɹ ɛ́:əðə
He used to go out to Felthorp Woods / gather heather.

58 jə dɨʔn nʌʊ ɛ́: ðɛɪd̚ bɨ́n dɨ́d ʒə

113

You didn't know where they'd been, did you?

59 ən əvéntʃɨɫ ða? fɫɜ́: fá·ɪə
And eventually that flew afire.

60 ɪi póɪnˀə t'ə mɪ́i ɪi sǽɪ | júu ɨnˀ gá:ˀ ə ɫʊ́ɪˀ
He pointed to me, he say / You ain't got a light.

61 ðə gɹáünd stá?t sʌ́dənɫɨ ðɛ: ən ðë̀ wəz ə stɹ́ip ɨ̊ŋkɫɒɪn̥ n̥ɛn ə
62 ɹɔ́: ə t'ɛ́ɹəst áüzəz
The ground stopped suddenly there and there was a steep incline then a row of terraced houses.

63 ən ˀɛ́vɹi á:f dǽɪ | ɨg góω ˀ ɹə dɨ́fɹənˀ skóωɫ n t'ɛ́:k' t'ű ə
64 θɹíi dɨ́fɹəŋˀ kɫá:səz
And every half-day / he'd go to a different school and take two or three different classes.

65 ɨn̥ ðə k'ɔ́:s əv ə jɛ́: jə lá:s t'üu jɛ́əz əˀ skóωɫ jə gá?
66 əbaü? θɹíi ɔ fɔ́: dɹɔ́:ɹən lɛ́sənz ə jɛ́ə
In the course of a year your last two years at school you got about three or four drawing lessons a year.

67 ðæɪ ɔ́:ɫ ɛd ə t'á: wɨð ə bɛ́ɫ ɨn
They all had a tower with a bell in.

68 ɒɪ θɨŋg̊ ˀaˀ wz ə k'ɨ́ɫ ɔ: k'ɜ́: düu ɹɛ́əɫɨ | ɨn̥ n̥ə sɔ́:mə
I think that was a kill or cure do, really / In the summer.

69 ðə t'ɹɪ́its jüus tə kɫá:ʃ | a:n ə θɜ́:zdɪ a:fˀnón
The treats used to clash / on a Thursday afternoon.

70 lɨ́ˀɫ óωɫz ɨn̥ n̥ə bǽ:k ə ðɨ ɛ́·ɪɫz | ɪ́i jüs tə səpɫʊ́ɪ ɔ:ɫ ɫə
71 mət'ɛ́:ɹɨəɫz | ən ɪi kɫɪ́əd̥ ðɛm ɔ́:ɫ aüˀ | ðə wómən ʃɹʌ́k áü?
Little holes in the back of the heels. / He used to supply all the materials. / And he cleared them all out. / The woman shruck out.

114

72 ðæɪ tˈɔ́ˀ mɨ́ ˀə ðə dʒɛ́·nə l̰ɨ́nd áü?pˈɛ́:ʃən?s dɨpˈá:?mən? ɨn
73 pʊ́:dɨgəˀ

They took me to the Jenny Lind out-patients department in Pottergate.

(iv) *Phonological discussion*
This speaker's phonological system is quite different in many respects from those of the other informants. The vowel system has more distinctions, reflecting earlier stages of English. Thus the following distinctions are made, though it must be pointed out that not all speakers in Norwich necessarily make them, especially the younger generations.

(a) /æɪ/ in *staithe* versus /ɛ̣:/ in *lane*. The latter is kept distinct from /ɛ:/ in *there, here* (see (d) below).
(b) /üu/ in *through* versus /oɷ/ in *go, school, no* versus /ʌɷ/ in *shoulder*.
(c) Some reflexes of ME ẹ̄ may be retained in words like *heel* with [e·ɪ] (70), as opposed to /ɪi/ in *three* (64).
(d) /ɪə/ and /ɛ:/ are kept apart, though there is some inconsistency in the realization of the former, e.g. [kɫɪəd̯] *cleared* (71), [ɛ:] *air* (28), but [jɛ:] (65) and [jẹ̣ə] (66) *year*, and [mətˈẹ̣:ɪɨətz] *materials* (71). *Here* (26) is pronounced with a slightly closer variety of vowel than *air* (28), making it the same as the vowel in *lane* (34). (For further comments on this distinction, see Trudgill and Foxcroft, 1978: 76-77.)
(e) /ɜ:/ has a variant /ɐ:/: compare *her* on lines (49) and (55), note also [ɨnvɐ:ˀəd] *inverted* (16). However, most words with /ɜ:/ in RP and other accents in E's speech have a short /ɐ/. There is no evidence to suggest that this is a synchronic vowel shortening process in that there are no alternant pronunciations, long : short.

The distribution of vowels in lexical items also varies more here than in the other accents. For example, /ɷ/, as in *put*, is also found in *boat, roast, poke, poker, bloke, most* and *stone* (cf. Trudgill, 1974: 72-73). Here again there is no evidence of a synchronic shortening. /a:/ occurs in *Harriet's* (49) and *clash* (69), as well as in the expected *last* and *heart*. In one instance *same*, which elsewhere has /ɛ̣:/, has the diphthong found in younger speakers in such words: [sæɪm dæɪ] *same day* (40). This could well be influence of the more recent pronunciation and the diphthong of the following word.

The glottal stop is a frequent realization of /t/, even in initial position of an unstressed syllable, e.g. [ʔə] *to* (33), (34), (37), (38), (72). On one occasion it occurs for /ð/: [ʔaʔ] *that* (68). It also occurs at the onset of a vowel, usually stressed, as in [ʔɑːp̥] *hop* (43), [ʔaːnʔ ʔaːɹɪəʔs] *Aunt Harriet's* (49) (cf. Trudgill, 1974: 182; see also below under Linking r). There are two instances of it as the realization of /k/: [ɫɑɪʔ] *like* (2), [t'ʊʔ] *took* (72), and one as the realization of /p/: [stɑʔt] *stopped* (61).

There is a distinction of /ʊ/ and /ʌ/, no /h/, no syllable-final /r/, and [ŋ] is not an underlying phonological unit. Before vowels we find unstressed final [i] as the realization of /ɨ/.

(a) *Lenition*. This process is not particularly widespread in E's speech, though there are number of examples of stop → fricative, as in:

[tʃʌx əʔ] *chuck it* (18)

[ðass] *that's* (30)

[bḛːçən] *bacon* (39) and (40)

[-bɑ·dɨ xəd] *-body could* (54).

(Note that the example on line (30) has not undergone Geminate Simplification.) Voicing of intervocalic voiceless stops is even less common in E's, though a number of Norwich speakers use it more often, e.g.

[pɒːdɨgəʔ] *Pottergate* (73).

[θɪŋg̊] *think* (68) is unusual; there is one instance of a flap: [pɔɾ əʔ] *put it* (21).

(b) *Harmony*. The alveolars /t d n/ in particular display place harmony, but in E's speech there are many examples where it does not occur, e.g.

[oʊpᵐz] *opens* (4)

[ən̪ n̪ə] *and the* (5) and (14)

[sʌft͡ʃ] *something* (7) and (47)

[ðæɪg gɨv] *they'd give* (12)

[ɹib bi] *he'd be* (23)

[dɨfɹənʔ kɫaːsəz] *different classes* (64)

[ad ðə] *had the* (14)

[ðɛɪd˺ bɨn] *they'd been* (58)

[daün ðɛ̈] *down there* (52)

[ɨnˀ gɑːˀ] *ain't got* (60).

/ð/-harmony also occurs, again with several exceptions, e.g.

[ən̥ n̥ə] *and the* (5) and (14)

[wɛ̈ ɬə] *well the* (11)

[ɔːɬ ɬə] *all the* (44) and (70)

[t'ɑɪm n̥ə] *time the* (52)

[lɛgz zə] *legs the* (55)

[ɨn ði] *in the* (25).

Voicing harmony occurs as well in [kos sæɪ] *course they* (39-40).

There is one instance of place harmony of /m/: [t'ɑɪɱ fə] *time for* (27). Nasalization of preceding vowels sometimes occurs: [kʌ̃nˀɹi] *country* (2), [ə̃m] *them* (12), [ə̃m̃n] *him* (23).

Palatal harmony is usual:

[mɒɪnd ʒüu] *mind you* (20)

[aʒ jü] *as you* (27)

[wəʒ jüʒəɬi] *was usually* (28)

[wɔnʃ jüud] *once you'd* (30)

[dɨd ʒə] *did you* (58).

(c) *CCS*. /t/ and /d/ are deleted in the usual circumstances, e.g.

[nɛks tüu] *next to* (11)

[ɹʌfəs p'ɬɛ̝ːs] *roughest place* (13)

[lɛf ʃʌɷɬdə] *left shoulder* (18)

[ɬɷk̚ daün] *looked down* (22)

[k'ʌɷɬ nɨp̚] *cold nip* (28).

In one instance the /t/ is retained where in most accents it is obligatory to delete it: [əɹʌp̚ɛ̝ʃn] *eruption* (54), in contrast to [ɹəfɬɛk̚ʃən] *reflection* (55).

The words *always* and *across* end in [st] before a vowel, but only [s] before a consonant, e.g.

[əkɹɔːst] (14), [ɔːɫwɨst] (16), [əkɹɔːs] (46), [ɔːɫəs] (51). Although this is epenthetic, historically speaking (cf. Strang, 1970: 166), the [t] can be treated as underlying in Norwich, subject to CCS as appropriate.

/n/ is sometimes deleted before /t/, realized as [ʔ], with no nasality of the vowel: [pˈɫɛʔi] *plenty* (47) (cf. Trudgill, 1974: 179).

Geminate Simplification occurs sporadically, e.g. [ɔːʃüu] (16), [wɛ̈ ɫə] (11).

(d) *UVD*. Unstressed vowels are often deleted under the same conditions as in the other localities, e.g.

[aü? ðæ?] *out of that* (23)

[ɛnɨ ði] *any of the* (34-35)

[ða? wz ʌɒnɨ] *that was only* (40)

[ɪi wz ʌɒni baü?] *he was only about* (42)

[bɨgɹ ən] *bigger than* (44).

There are also instances, less common elsewhere, such as:

[wɹivz] *weavers* (33)

[kˈæːbnə?] *cabinet* (56)

[aːfʔnɒn] *afternoon* (69).

Following a glottal stop, especially before another vowel, [ə] is deleted (cf. Stockport and Peasmarsh, above), e.g.

[bɑːðə ʔ aːsk] *bother to ask* (45)

[sʌft͡ʃ ʔ ɪi?] *something to eat* (47).

In conjunction with linking r, this gives forms such as [gɒɒ ʔ ɹə] *go to a* (63). In [tɚːm] *to them* (3) the linking r and the two unstressed vowels have merged into a long r-coloured vocoid. This merging of [ə] with a preceding vowel is discussed in detail by Trudgill (1974: 159-62). It applies both within and across word boundaries. There are not many instances of this in E's speech, but [flɜː faˑɹə] *flew afire* (59) is one. When word-final /r/ is realized as [ə], this too affects a preceding vowel; thus, we find the following derivation: /küur/ ⇒ küuə ⇒ [kˈɜː] *cure* (68). In E's speech we can see that this merging does not always take place, e.g. [tˈü ə] *two or* (63).

As a final example of UVD I shall take the unstressed sequence *going to* (38), showing the interaction with other rules:

/goʊən tüu/

Stress placement	⇒	goən tə
/t/-realization	⇒	goən ʔə
/n/-deletion	⇒	goə ʔə
UVD	⇒	[go ʔə].

(e) *Linking r*. As already mentioned in the Introduction, Norwich speakers extend the application of linking r, e.g.

[tɞ:m] *to them* (3)

[ɨnʔəɪ ə] *into a* (7)

[dɹɔ:ɪən] *drawing* (24) and (66)

[bəɪ a:ʔ] *by heart* (32)

[tᵊɵɪ ɛnɨ] *to any* (34)

[goʊ ʔ ɪə] *go to a* (63),

as well as in the expected environments, e.g. [wəɪ æ:pɨ] *were happy* (8). Alongside these there are also a few instances of [ʔ] used as a link, e.g. [tə ʔɑ:p] *to hop* (43).

(f) *Vowel lengthening*. It is necessary to differentiate those cases where vowel length is lexically determined from those where it is determined by the phonetic environment. On the one hand, words such as *last* and *off* always have a long vowel and are examples of the first type; on the other hand, *got* and *that* are found with both long and short vowel phases. In the latter category, stress plays an important role, but the following sound may also make it more likely that the vowel is lengthened. In particular the voiceless stops ([1]), the nasals and /r/ seem to influence vowel length, though it is also found before other sounds as well, e.g.

[nɑ:ɪɨdʒ] *Norwich* (5) and (37)

[ʃɑ:p] *shop* (7)

[æ:pɨ] *happy* (8)

[æ:ŋɨn] *hanging* (16)

[pʻɑ:ʔ] *pot* (23)

[wɒ:nʔ] *want* (25)

[bɑ:ðə] *bother* (45)

[sɑ:ŋ] *song* (51)

[kʻæːbnə?] *cabinet* (56)

[pɒːdɨgə?] *Pottergate* (73).

In one instance, [bɹɛ̝ːk̂fəst] (27), the vowel may be the reflex of what was originally a long vowel anyway, even though it was shortened in most accents. Without evidence in the form of alternative pronunciations with long and short vowel phases in this speaker, it is difficult to determine to what extent length is the result of a synchronic or a past process. More data would be needed to come to any firm conclusions regarding this somewhat complex phenomenon in Norwich speech. It may also be that there is a correlation between the last stressed syllable in a breath group and this type of lengthening, except in the case of the high vowels /ɨ/ and /ɞ/, though again there is insufficient evidence here to come to any firm conclusions.

NOTES

([1]) It is interesting to note that this lengthening before voiceless sounds is opposite to what is found in RP and some other accents (cf. Gimson, 1962: 90-91) and to what is normally interpreted as "natural" (cf. Hyman, 1975: 172).

Chapter Seven

COMPARISON AND DISCUSSION

This chapter is a preliminary phonological statement and interpretation of the data presented in the individual localities. I hope to show the main similarities and differences between the six accents and indicate how these can be handled in terms of rules. In the final section I shall indicate those areas which, in the light of recent developments in phonological theory, need further investigation.

THE MODEL CHOSEN
First of all, it is necessary to present the model of description chosen. For the most part, I have followed Brown's (1972) scheme. Since I am not concerned with morphological alternations, Brown's simpler model (than, for example, Chomsky and Halle's) is more suited to my purposes (cf. Brown's comments, 1972: 26-28). In particular, I want to argue in favour of underlying elements specified only in terms of non-redundant features and against the systematic phonemic level. Lexical representations are concerned with the distinctive features of the language in question, the redundant ones being supplied by the redundancy rules. Thus in English /f/ differs from the other voiceless fricatives in that it is labial, just as /p/ differs from the other voiceless stops. The fact that the former is labiodental and the latter bilabial is a matter of phonetic precision, not phonological contrasts: /f/ does not contrast with any other voiceless labiodental consonant in English, nor does /p/ contrast with any other voiceless bilabial. (Contrast this with the fricatives of Ewe; Ladefoged, 1982: 144.) Furthermore, what is distinctive varies from context to context. In English a nasal before a stop will be homorganic with that stop, e.g. [lɪmp], [lɪnt], [lɪŋk], so that place of articulation

is not a distinguishing feature of the nasals in
this position, since it is entirely dependent on the
following stop ([1]). This has led some linguists to
establish an unspecified nasal /N/ in such cases in
English and other languages (cf. Fudge, 1969b;
Trudgill, 1974; Brown, 1972). The fully specified
systematic phonemic level may well equate to a body
of knowledge based partly on the spelling system,
which in English is morphophonemic in character, and
also related to a certain amount of taught, conscious
knowledge. That is to say, firstly, some of the
underlying forms incorporate morphophonemic information, as often reflected in the spelling, which
has to be learnt more or less consciously and which
may not be available to all speakers to the same
degree. Secondly, especially as far as learned
vocabulary is concerned, knowledge of sets of related
words with alternating stem vowels and/or final
consonants is distributed very variously throughout
the native speakers of English (cf. also Cutler's,
1980, investigations referred to in the Introduction).
However, even in phonetic terms, the full specification of underlying segments may not be justified,
when consideration is given to language in the context
of its use. To quote Brown (1972: 46), a theory of
redundancy in the phonological component of a grammar
"must surely be to account, for instance, for the
perception of utterances which are masked by a high
degree of noise. The problem is one of identifying
the minimum input necessary for interpretation of an
utterance. It is a highly redundant theory of phonology which insists that a minimally redundant acoustic
input must always be processed (or indeed produced)
by stringing together fully specified systematic
phonemes and taking no account of the word, or message,
in which they appear.". Of course, the final sound
of *cat* and the initial sound of *tack* have to be
identified as the same, if this reflects the native
speaker's knowledge satisfactorily, but the resultant
/t/ does not have to be specified as:

      [- vocalic]
      [+ consonantal]
      [- high]
      [- back]
      [- low]
      [+ anterior]
      [+ coronal]
      [- voice]
      [- continuant]

[- nasal]
[- strident]

(or with any equivalent set of phonetic specifications) simply because it is pronounced that way in initial position, or in some kind of standard, careful speech. It is quite conceivable that many native speakers of English never pronounce final post-vocalic /t/ as anything but [ʔ].

In addition to Brown's arguments against the systematic phonemic level (1972: 41-46), we may also wish to argue that the unspecified nature of certain features in the lexical entry forms reflects the knowledge that native speakers have as to which sounds harmonize and which do not. In the case of the alveolars, so-called, the place of articulation varies considerably, as we have already seen. We can reflect this fact by leaving /t/, /d/ and /n/ unspecified for place and having process and realization rules to supply the appropriate feature. Differentiation of place in the alveolar stops and nasal may be more of a consciously learnt aspect of the phonological system for some speakers of English, in particular, those who use harmonized forms a great deal (cf. Newton's (1970) and Ferguson's (1978) comments on Modern Greek, a language which also displays a lot of interword consonantal harmony in colloquial speech)(^{2}). It is interesting to note that English, in many of its accents, shows what can be interpreted as the first stage in final voiceless stop loss found in a number of other languages (eg. Thai, Mandarin, Maori). Voiceless stops harmonize with following sounds, add a glottal closure, loose the supraglottal closure, retaining only the glottal one, and finally loose the closure altogether. (See also Aitchison's discussion of this, 1981: 132-33.) Such a change can be explained by progressive feature loss in the underlying specifications (see below for further discussion). In the English accents under consideration (with the possible exception of Edinburgh, see Chapter 4 above) so far only the place feature has disappeared from the underlying specification of the "alveolars".

The underlying (i.e. occurring in lexical entries) stops and nasals in all the accents under consideration in this book have the following specifications, using Ladefoged's system of feature classification (1982: 254-66):

	/p/	/t/	/k/	/b/
	[-voice]	[-voice]	[-voice]	[+voice]
	[stop]	[stop]	[stop]	[stop]
	[labial]	[Øplace]	[velar]	[-nasal]
				[labial]

	/d/	/g/	/m/	/n/
	[+voice]	[+voice]	[Øvoice]	[Øvoice]
	[stop]	[stop]	[stop]	[stop]
	[-nasal]	[-nasal]	[+nasal]	[+nasal]
	[Øplace]	[velar]	[labial]	[Øplace]

whereby Ø = unspecified, to be accounted for by a later rule. As mentioned above, in Edinburgh the informants use harmony less than in the other localities, so that it might be more appropriate for the feature [alveolar] to appear at this stage to mark the accent off as different in this respect. This would then make the harmony rule (see below) different for these informants. However, since more data would be needed before a more definite decision could be made on this point, I shall leave the underlying specifications the same for all the accents, thereby simplifying the statement of the harmony rule.

Redundancy rules, in the form of *if-then* conditions, account for the specification of [+voice] for the nasals and [-nasal] for the voiceless stops:

```
If   [+nasal]          If   [-voice]
       ⇓                       ⇓
then [+voice]          then [-nasal]
```

The fricatives have the following specifications:

	/f/	/θ/	/s/	/ʃ/
	[-voice]	[-voice]	[-voice]	[-voice]
	[fric]	[fric]	[fric]	[fric]
	[labial]	[dental]	[alv]	[palatal]

	/v/	/ð/	/z/	/ʒ/
	[+voice]	[+voice]	[+voice]	[+voice]
	[fric]	[Ømanner]	[fric]	[fric]
	[labial]	[dental]	[alv]	[palatal]

The phonetic detail that /f/ and /v/ are realized as labiodental by most speakers is a matter of a redundancy rule of the form:

> If [fric]
>   [labial]
>   ⇓
> then [dental]

We may note that Y has an optional harmony rule whereby [labial] sounds in her system may be bilabial or labiodental depending on adjacent sounds, whether stop or fricative (cf. Chapter 1 above). /ʃ/ and /ʒ/ have the feature [alv] added to their specifications by redundancy rule. This gives all instances of [ʃ] and [ʒ] the same phonetic specification whether underlying or a result of palatal harmony (cf. Lodge, 1981: 27-28).

The unspecified manner feature of /ð/ reflects the widespread harmony to which this segment is subject. In all the accents under consideration the manner of articulation of /ð/ is determined by the following sounds, as exemplified in the chapters above.

The affricates /tʃ/ and /dʒ/ are members of the stop series with the underlying place feature [palatal] as with /ʃ/ and /ʒ/; a redundancy rule accounts for the fricative release and the [alv] specification. Palatal harmony of /t/ and /d/ involves copying the feature [palatal] to their underlying specification with the same results (see below for details).

/l/, /w/ and /j/ can be specified as follows:

/l/	/w/	/j/
[approx]	[approx]	[approx]
[alv]	[labial]	[palatal]

The phonetic characteristics of /r/ are not the same for each locality, though the rules which apply to it may be (cf. Introduction, p. 13). Therefore, if we wish to have the rules applicable to all accents as appropriate, the specification of /r/ must be sufficiently wide to cover the diverse realizations. Since trills and approximants do not have many phonetic characteristics in common, we can resort to the pseudo-phonetic feature [liquid] (cf. Ladefoged, 1982: 86) to reflect the phonological character of /r/, and its behaviour in syllable structure along with /l/, /j/ and /w/ (cf. Lass, 1976: 18). [liquid] could then replace [approx] in the above specifications and /r/ could be given an unspecified manner feature:

```
        /w/        /l/        /r/        /j/
      [liquid]   [liquid]   [liquid]   [liquid]
      [labial]   [alv]      [Ømanner]  [palatal]
```

The redundancy rules for /r/ would then be different for each variant, depending on the realization involved. Thus, speaker Y would have a rule:

```
    If    [liquid]
          [Ømanner]
             ⇓
    then  [approx]
          [labial]
          [dental]
```

whereas B would have:

```
    If    [liquid]
          [Ømanner]
             ⇓
    then  [approx]
          [retracted].
```

Some speakers have variant realizations of /r/, e.g. G, H and E, for which variable rules may be necessary (cf. Romaine's, 1978, treatment of /r/ in Edinburgh).

We should note in connection with Ø-specifications of features that the redundancy rules have to be understood in such a way that the feature specified Ø disappears from the segment in question when the redundant features are written in. This is because within the Ladefoged system of classification the features given Ø-specifications are hyponyms of the redundant features; [place] and [manner] are not features like [labial], [+voice], and [stop], but are major class categories.

The vowels are rather more complicated than the consonants, as there is much more variety in terms of realization in the former. I shall not attempt a full analysis of them here, but there are a few aspects of the system which should be noted.

Lip-rounding, which is traditionally associated with vowels (eg. Gimson, 1962), is not a distinctive feature of the English vowel system; there are no vowel contrasts carried solely by the opposition rounded versus unrounded. It can be accounted for by the redundancy rules. In Norwich it is associated with certain consonants in some instances, so that non-high back vowels, which are elsewhere unrounded, take on lip-rounding after bilabial consonants (cf.

Chapter 6 above)(³).

The main aspect of the vowel system I want to consider is the status of length and the interpretation of diphthongs. In RP and some other accents of English vowel length is not distinctive (cf. Ladefoged, 1982: 84, 87 and 225). It is determined by the voice characteristics of the following consonant, and in the context of an utterance the amount of stress placed on a particular syllable affects the length of the vowel. Of the accents presented here, only Edinburgh has no length distinction (cf. Lass, 1976: 31); in fact, length is much more restricted here than in RP. The other accents have contrastive length, though the matter is not straightforward in Norwich (see Chapter 6 above). The difference in the occurrence of length in part accounts for the rhythmic differences between the accents and may be a matter of variant realizations of the same underlying units. The two questions to be answered are: (i) Should the common underlying vowels be specified as long or short? (ii) Are the diphthongs a separate category?

Let us start with the second of these questions. Traditional descriptions of RP (e.g. Gimson, 1962) analyse the diphthongs as separate from the other vowel phonemes, whereas descriptions of American English by American linguists (e.g. Trager and Smith, 1951; Hockett, 1958; Chomsky and Halle, 1968) interpret them as vowel + glide; thus the vowel phase of *gate* is /eɪ/ or /ey/ respectively (ignoring the more complex SPE analysis for the moment). The vowels of *feet* and *food* are also treated differently: /iː/ and /uː/ on the one hand, and /iy/ and /uw/ on the other. Lass (1976: 3-39) has argued at length for assigning long vowels and diphthongs to the same phonological class in English, namely vowel cluster (/VV/), the difference between the two being "simply a matter of identity or nonidentity of nuclear constituents" (ibid.: 22). He dismisses the category <u>glide</u> in English phonology as a misinterpretation of the phonetic facts of the end point of the diphthongal movements (ibid.: 15-19), as well as demonstrating that the SPE feature of tenseness is nothing more than a convenient abstraction (ibid.: esp. 39-50)(⁴). To these arguments he adds as further support that such an analysis utilizing vowel clusters helps us to give a simpler account of the historical process of diphthongization of earlier long monophthongs (and, incidentally, the less commonly discussed monophthongization of earlier diphthongs, cf. ibid.: 32) than the

SPE account does, and enables us to give phonetically
disparate accents the same dichotomous distinction
in the vowels: /V/ versus /VV/. If we accept Lass's
arguments (and his evidence is compelling), then the
accents presented here, with the exception of Edinburgh, all have the /V/ - /VV/ distinction, whether
or not /VV/ represents long monophthongs or diphthongs ([5]).

Given the /V/ - /VV/ distinction, we can now
answer the first question as to the nature of the
common underlying vowels. Historically, all accents
of English appear to have had a long - short distinction in the vowels, and this is what is still preserved
in the accents described here, with altered realizations.
Table 1 gives the equivalences for the Middle English
long vowels.

TABLE 1

ME	S	SB	P	C	N
i:	/aː/~/ae/	/ɑɪ/	/ɑɪ/	/ɔɪ/	/ɑɪ/
e:	/eɪ/	/ɪi/	/ɪi/	/ɪi/	/ɪi/
a:	/eː/~/ɛɪ/	/ɛɪ/	/ɛɪ/	/ɛɪ/	/ɛ̝ː/
u:	/æɷ/	/æɷ/	/æɷ/	/æɷ/	/ɑü/
o:	/ɪɷ/~/ou/	/ɷu/	/ɷu/	/ɷu/	/oɷ/*
ɔ:	/oː/~/ʌɷ/	/ʌɷ/	/ʌɷ/	/ʌɷ/	/üu/*

(The localities are represented by their initials.)

*The distribution of these sounds is somewhat compli-
cated in Norwich, and involves /ɷ/ as well (cf.
Trudgill, 1974: 72-73 and Trudgill and Foxcroft, 1978).

We can see from this that the /VV/ specification
remains intact in each accent. If we take this as
the basic form, accents such as Edinburgh will have
to be subject to a shortening rule: $V_x V_x = V_x$, where x
is a set of feature specifications.

The final point about the vowel system that I
wish to make is the status of [ə] in the underlying
representations. Where there are stress alternations,
as in *photograph - photography*, [ə] is derivable from
an appropriate full vowel by the stress placement
rules. This would mean that in speaker Y's system
the base morpheme *photograph*, for instance, would
have the lexical entry form: /fʌɷtɑgraf/. On the
other hand, where there are no stress alternations,
as in *about*, the underlying representation will have

/ə/ as the initial vowel(⁶). In Table 4 below, none of the accents under consideration has word-final /ə/ in words such as *carter*, *farmer*, etc., but those forms of RP without any linking r do (cf. the Introduction above, p. 14).

COMPARISON
In the preceding section I have outlined what the accents under discussion have in common. We must now turn to a consideration of the differences between the accents and formalize the process rules which have been discussed above in the separate chapters. In order to try to establish degrees of difference, the following types of accent differentiation are assumed: (1) variation in the number of phonological contrasts, e.g. the vowels of *put* and *putt* distinguished or not; (2) variation in the incidence of the phonological units in lexical items, e.g. *book* and *pool* with the same or different vowels; (3) application of processes in different ways, e.g. *letter* with intervocalic [s] or [d]; (4) phonetic realization differences, e.g. /r/ as [ʋ] or [ɹ], and rhythmic differences related to syllable length; (5) phonotactic differences, e.g. whether or not /r/ can occur before consonants; (6) differences in articulatory setting, e.g. tense versus lax musculature. The different parts of the grammar involved in pinpointing differences in accent reflect to some extent the amount to which native speakers are consciously aware of them. For example, people are most conscious of the differences located in the underlying segments, such as lack of the /ɒ/-/ʌ/ distinction and lack of /h/. Similarly, lexical incidence and distributional differences (as in Tables 3 and 4 below) tend to be recognized, since they too involve segments and their arrangement. On the other hand, phonetic differences, which involve only one or two features, or a redundancy rule, are less likely to be consciously picked out, and processes such as harmony are very often totally ignored.

   Table 2 is a comparison of the systematic differences displayed by the informants under consideration in this book, as far as the vowels are concerned. (The localities are indicated by initial.)

TABLE 2

S	SB	P	E	C	N
/ɛe/ ⎫ /e:/ ⎭	/ɛɪ/	/ɛɪ/	/e/	/ɛɪ/	/æɪ/ /ɛ̣:/
/o:/	/ʌɷ/	/ʌɷ/	/o/	/ʌɷ/	/ʌɷ/ /oɷ/
/ʉu/	/ɷu/	/ɷu/	/u/	/ɷu/	/üu/
/o/ ⎰ /ɷ/ /ʌ/	/ɷ/ /ʌ/	/ɷ/ /ʌ/	/ʌ/	/ɷ/ /ʌ/	/ɷ/ /ʌ/

NB: The /ɛe/:/e:/ distinction does not apply to speaker Y, who also has a diphthong /ʌɷ/ rather than /o:/, and /ɪɷ/ rather than /ʉu/. Norwich /æɪ/ is not the equivalent of Stockport /ɛe/, having a different historical origin.

The distinctions found only in one or two accents, indicated by braced pairs in Table 2, show the extent to which the underlying vowel systems differ at this fundamental level. In other respects the systems of the accents under discussion are the same, as far as the underlying units are concerned.
   Table 3 gives examples of differences in lexical incidence.

TABLE 3

	S	SB	P	E	C	N
last	/a/	/ɑ:/	/a:/	/a:/	/a/~/a:/	/a:/
book	/ʉu/(N)	/ɷ/	/ɷ/	/u/	/ɷ/	/ɷ/
boat	/o:/(N)	/ʌɷ/	/ʌɷ/	/o/	/ʌɷ/	/ɷ/
cart	/a:/	/ɑ:/	/ar/	/ar/	/a:/	/a:/
serve	/ø:/	/ə:/	/er/	/ɛr/	/e:/	/ɐ:/~/3:/
church	/ø:/	/ə:/	/er/	/ʌr/	/e:/	/ɐ/
more	/oə/(N) /ɔ:/(Y)	/ɔ:/	/ɔr/	/or/	/ɔ:/	/ɔ:/
sort	/ɔ:/	/ɔ:/	/ɔr/	/ɔr/	/ɔ:/	/ɔ:/
tall	/ɔ:/	/ɔ:/	/ɔ:/	/ɔ/	/ɔ:/	/ɔ:/

NB: Speaker Y often uses an unrounded form of /ɔ:/.

The consonantal systems are less varied, but we have noted that /h/ is usually not an underlying unit. /ng/ is realized differently in different accents, but this is a matter of rule variation (see below). Similarly, /r/ may occur post-vocalically before a consonant or it may be restricted from occurring in that position, as described in the Introduction (pp. 12-14); this is a matter of lexical incidence. Table 4 gives a number of underlying forms for words involving historical /r/.

TABLE 4

	S	SB	P	E	C	N
car	/kaːr/	/kɑːr/	/kar/	/kar/	/kaːr/	/kaːr/
cart	/kaːt/	/kɑːt/	/kart/	/kart/	/kaːt/	/kaːt/
carter	/kaːtr̩/	/kɑːtr̩/	/kartr̩/	/kartr̩/	/kaːtr̩/	/kaːtr̩/

THE PROCESS RULES

I now want to consider the rules for handling the phonological processes discussed in the individual chapters and compare their application across the six accents. I shall start with the stops and consider harmony and glottal reinforcement. The following redundancy rules account for the harmony of /t/, /d/ and /n/, and their specification as [alveolar] elsewhere.

1. If [stop]
      [Øplace]
         ⇓
      then [αplace]/ _____   C
                            [αplace]

2. If [stop]
      [Øplace]
         ⇓
      then [alv]

The rules cannot be collapsed because 1 is optional and 2 obligatory, and 2 must apply even in the context specified in 1, if the latter does not apply. The rules have to account for the fact that /d/ in *good man* can be realised as [b] or [d], whilst in *good evening* it must be [d]. (See also footnote 10 of this chapter.)

Glottal reinforcement involves a change in

phonation type (cf. Ladefoged, 1982: 258). In English the basic distinction is between those sounds that have voice and those that do not. The third possibility - simultaneous glottal stop - is a derived (i.e. not basic) articulation of the voiceless series in certain contexts. (The glottal stop is neither voiced nor voiceless because of the position of the vocal cords; it is, however, 'without voice'.) Rule 3 accounts for glottal reinforcement.

3. [-voice] ⇒ [glottal]/ ___ $ (opt.)
[stop]

The context specifies syllable-final position. In most accents this occurs before another consonant or a pause, not before a vowel. This is because a following vowel requires syllable overlap, that is the segment in question is ambisyllabic, whether underlying or derived by concatenation in the speech chain(⁷). Thus, *city* and *got a* have the following syllable structure, using a dependency notation (see Anderson, ms):

Glottal reinforcement cannot apply in cases of overlap as indicated by the environment template, where the syllable boundary follows the stop segment. However, in Norwich we do find intervocalic reinforced stops, so that only in word-initial position are they ruled out. We, therefore, need to posit a different underlying syllable structure for words like *city* for those speakers who always have glottally reinforced stops (or glottal realization of /t/, see below). This means no overlapping, and resyllabification via concatenation does not take place either, i.e.

If there are alternating forms with and without glottal reinforcement, then we need a rule of resyllabification under certain circumstances. I shall discuss this further below, when I consider variation in glottal realization of /t/. (See also footnote 8 of this chapter.)

We now have to account for the occurrence of [?] only as the realization of /t/. Rule 4 has slightly different contexts for its operation as shown below. Table 5 indicates how these alternative versions of the rule are distributed in my informants' speech.

    4. [-voice] ⇒ [glottal]/ _____ (C)$ (opt.)
       [∅place]   [+voice][stop]

as in *hit, went, cotton, Scotland, got a*, but not **first, *loft, *centre, *bottle, *petrol, *better, *ten*. The difference between *cotton* with [?] and *bottle, petrol* with [t] is one of syllabification. In the former instance underlying /t/ must be syllable-final, whereas in the latter examples the /t/ is ambisyllabic and therefore does not fit the environment template. Intervocalic /t/ is also excluded from the environment specification in that it, too, is ambisyllabic.

    4'.   / _____ (C)$ C
                  [+voice][stop]

The inclusion of the rightmost C excludes examples such as *got a* from glottal realization.

    4''.   / _____ (C)$
                 [stop]

4'' allows words with a voiceless sound before /t/, e.g. *afternoon, lost* to be subject to the rule. In each case rule 4 is subject to the condition that the stress immediately following /t/ is not greater than the stress immediately preceding it (cf. Leslie, ms).

In cases where /k/ is realized as [?] we need rule 5.

    5. [-voice] ⇒ [glottal]/ V _____ (#)C
       [velar]   [stop]

as in *picture, took me* but not **kicker, *took it, *think*. I shall return to a consideration of glottal reinforcement and glottal realization below, when I discuss lenition and related processes.

The above rules do not allow glottal reinforcement of word-initial /t/ and /k/ or glottal realization, but we must note the following examples:

    [spo:s ? beɪ] *supposed to be* Stockport (75)
    [jɐu k̬] *you can* Peasmarsh (26)

[ʌp ʔ sɪi] *up to see* Peasmarsh (43)

[jɔ k�] *you can* Coventry (58)

[daün ʔə] *down to* Norwich (34)

[bɑːðə ʔ ɑːsk] *bother to ask* Norwich (45).

In such cases the syllable structure has been changed by unstressed vowel reduction or deletion, so that the /t/ and /k/ take up syllable positions where they can be realized as [ʔ]. In cases such as *you can* and *down to* the initial /k/ and /t/ belong to both syllables:

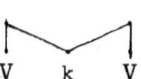 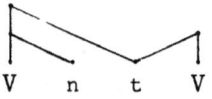

If the stops retain their ambisyllabicity, they are realized as oral stops. If, however, they become the final consonants of the first syllable and become detached from the second one, they are realized as [ʔ]. The same process accounts for H's alternations of [t] and [ʔ] in words like *centre*:

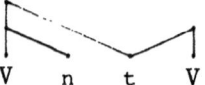 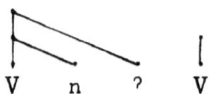

In some instances the operation of UVD produces the same end of syllable positions, eg.

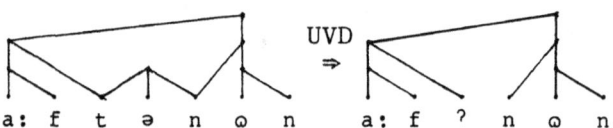

This is a Norwich pronunciation (line 69); I have not included the detail of /aː/. If there is no alternation between [t] and [ʔ], but the surface form is always [ʔ], then the underlying form must have a syllable-final /t/ not an ambisyllabic one([8]), as suggested above in relation to glottal reinforcement in Norwich.

This brings us to the examples involving the infinitive particle *to* (*to-inf*) and, in Stockport only, the definite article. In Norwich a form such as [jüs ʔə] (57) is accounted for by rule 4'' after the syllable structure has been altered, because

there is no reference to the voice characteristics of
the preceding environment. However, this is not the
case with 4 and 4', where voiceless sounds are
excluded from the environment template. Therefore,
supposed to be and *up to see* in the above examples
should be excluded from glottal realization according
to the rule. In those accents that allow glottal
realization in such cases it is only with *to*-inf, not
prepositional *to*. Thus, *supposed to be* above is
well-formed, whereas

$$*[\text{klo:s ? bɛɹe}] \quad close\ to\ Bury$$

is not. In Stockport we can add the glottal realization of *the* to these examples, as the only other
morpheme involved in such environments, e.g.

$$[\text{pas ? saɫt}] \quad pass\ the\ salt,$$

but not $\quad *[\text{pas? ə beskeʔ}] \quad passed\ a\ biscuit.$

In Chapter 1 I suggested a possible treatment
for the glottal realization of *the*, which can be
revised in the light of the preceding discussion of
glottal realization. *The* and *to*-inf are exceptions
and will have to be treated so. One way to do this
would be to have a 'dummy' underlying preceding
[+voice] in the lexical entry for these two words;
thus:

$$/_{[+\text{voice}]}\text{tV}/ \quad to\text{-inf}$$

$$/_{[+\text{voice}]}\text{θV}/ \quad the$$

(where the exact specification of V is irrelevant).
The dummy voice specification would then have to be
deleted, as follows:

6. $[+\text{voice}] \Rightarrow \emptyset\ /\ [-\text{voice}]\_\_\_\_[\text{glottal}]$ (obl.)

This gives the following derivations:

$$/\text{pas}_{[+\text{voice}]}\text{θV sɑlt}/ \quad /\text{ʌp}_{[+\text{voice}]}\text{tV sɪi}/$$

Stress
placement $\Rightarrow \text{pas}_{[+\text{voi}]}\text{θə sɑlt} \quad\quad \text{ʌp}_{[+\text{voi}]}\text{tə sɪi}$

t-insertion $\Rightarrow \text{pas}_{[+\text{voi}]}\text{tθə sɑlt} \quad\quad$ ——

UVD $\Rightarrow \text{pas}_{[+\text{voi}]}\text{tθ sɑlt} \quad\quad \text{ʌp}_{[+\text{voi}]}\text{t sɪi}$

θ-deletion $\Rightarrow \text{pas}_{[+\text{voi}]}\text{t sɑlt} \quad\quad$ ——

4 $\Rightarrow \text{pas}_{[+\text{voi}]}\text{? sɑlt} \quad\quad \text{ʌp}_{[+\text{voi}]}\text{? sɪi}$

6 ⇒ [pas ? saɫt]   [ʌp ? sɪi]

Even the absolute initial instances could be accounted for in this way, if we alter the environment of rule 6 to include a pause (∅):

6. [+voice] ⇒ ∅ / {[-voice]} ___[glottal](obl.).
              {   ∅   }

Table 5 gives a comparison of rule application for the voiceless stops.

TABLE 5

S	SB	P	E	C	N
1	1	1	1	1	1
2	2	2	2	2	2
3	3	3	3	3	3
4(Y) 4'(N)	4	4'	4	4'	4''
5(Y)	5	6	5(H)		5
6(N)					

In Norwich rule 6 is unnecessary, because the context is covered by the extended template of 4'', as mentioned above. The differences in glottal realization distribution are determined by what we may refer to as the operation of Right Release (RR), that is the loss of a right subjunction by an ambisyllabic /t/, as described above. In Norwich and speaker H in Edinburgh RR is applied far more frequently than in the other informants, e.g. *city* is usually:

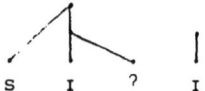

s ɪ ? ɪ

Y uses it very occasionally, as in [bɛ?ə] (41). Speaker N occasionally uses rule 4, as in [gɑ?] + V (84), rather than 4'. In formal terms this means that the environment template of 4' loses its rightmost C.

We can now turn to a consideration of CCS and some other instances of deletion. CCS can be given as rule 7:

7. [αvoice]   ⇒ ∅ /   C   +C   (opt.)
   [stop]   [αvoice]
   [-nasal]

where + is a morpheme boundary. This deletes a stop,
mostly /t/ and /d/, in the appropriate environment.
Similarly, /k/ is deleted in /-sk+/ sequences, and
in those accents where /ng/ is realized as [ŋg] /g/
also deletes, as in [θeŋz], Stockport (36). The
specification [-nasal] excludes /-lm/ and /-ln/
sequences from the rule(⁹). In Edinburgh /r/ must
be excluded from the preceding context, since the
/d/ in *word*, for example, does not delete before a
consonant. In this respect /r/ acts differently
from its fellow liquid /l/, and can even precede /l/
to produce three-consonant clusters not permitted
in non-rhotic accents; words such as *world*, *words*
are not subject to CCS.

/n/ is different from the non-nasal stops and
must be dealt with by separate rules, even though
in the individual localities I included it under CCS.
In some accents a word like *want* may have any of the
following pronunciations (with the appropriate vowel
quality, which is irrelevant to the present point):
[wɑnt], [wɑ̃nt], [wɑnʔ], [wɑ̃nʔ], [wɑʔ], [wɑ̃ʔ], though
they do not all occur in all the accents under
discussion here. To account for all these forms we
need the optional rules 8 and 9.

8.   V   ⇒   V   / ___ C   (opt.)
              [+nasal]   [+nasal]

9.   [stop]   ⇒   ∅   / V ___ ʔ#   (opt.)
     [+nasal]

These give us the following possible derivations
each stage of which is a possible pronunciation:

```
            /wɑnt/                    /wɑnt/
8  ⇒        [wɑ̃nt]           4  ⇒    [wɑnʔ]
4  ⇒        [wɑ̃nʔ]           9  ⇒    [wɑʔ]
9  ⇒        [wɑ̃ʔ]
```

None of the accents presented here allow 9 to apply
before [t]. In Edinburgh neither speaker has rules
8 and 9, and only H has rule 6. Neither of the
Peasmarsh informants has rules 8 and 9 either. In
Stockport speaker Y extends the context of rule 9
to include alveolar fricatives and a pause, e.g.
[ẽ st-] (10), [t'ø̃ːz] (11), [ðɛ̃] (7). In [ə̃ m-] (34),
as in [wɛ̃ m-] Coventry (68), Place Harmony and
Geminate Simplification have been applied (cf. p.106
above). In Shepherd's Bush too, speaker C has
extended the context to both alveolar and dental
fricatives, e.g. [mɑĩz] (5), [ṽ ðə] (28), [sɑ̃θɪŋk̰](48).

There are also examples in her speech of rule 9 being applied to [ʔ] = /k/, e.g. [əɪ̃ʔ] (5) and (9).

I have already discussed /g/-deletion in Chapters 1 and 2 above to account for [ŋ] without a following velar stop, but in fact it is less straightforward than just a simple deletion rule. The rules involved apply in other environments in some of the accents under discussion. First we need a rule for left-to-right voicing harmony, as in [wɛnt] ⇒ [wɛnd]:

    10. [-voice] ⇒ [+voice] / [+nasal] ___ #
                                         [stop]

(This may be seen as an instance of lenition.) Then we need a rule for left-to-right nasal harmony, as in [wɛnd] ⇒ [wɛnn]:

    11. [-nasal] ⇒ [+nasal] / [+nasal] ___ #
                                         [+voice]
                                         [stop]

These two rules would also apply to the sequence /ng/, so we have the following derivations:

		/wɛnt/	/sɛnd/	/sɪng/
1	⇒	wɛnt	sɛnd	sɪŋg
10	⇒	wɛnd	———	———
11	⇒	wɛnn	sɛnn	sɪŋŋ

Geminate Simplification, rule 12, can now be applied to the outputs of rule 11.

    12. C_i ⇒ ∅ / C_i ___ (opt.)

where i is a set of feature specifications.

    12 ⇒ [wɛn]   [sɛn]   [sɪŋ]

At this point we may note that some of the rules are optional in some circumstances and obligatory in others, even in the same accent([10]). For example, *went* and *send* can have any of the stages shown in the derivation above as surface forms in Shepherd's Bush, but only the output of rules 11 and 12 in Peasmarsh, which means that in the latter locality rule 11 is obligatory, if rule 10 is chosen([11]). On the other hand, /sɪng/ is subject to all three rules in all the accents except Stockport. It is true that historical changes can be handled quite satisfactorily in terms of rules spreading, retreating or being lost altogether. In the case under discussion /-mb/ has been eliminated from English by these rules, /-ng/ not quite, because of the alternations such as *long - longer*, and /-nd/ is least affected. However, there are other considerations from a synchronic point of view. The difference between optional and obligatory application of rules in this particular case may indicate that we should postulate an underlying /ŋ/ in words like *sing* which have no morphological alternations([12]).

If we take /ng/ as the underlying form of [ŋ], we can explain the different pronunciations of *length* with final [-ŋθ] or [-n̪θ], which varies from person to person rather than locality to locality. These forms can be accounted for in terms of different ordering in the application of rules 1 and 7, giving the following derivations:

		/leng+θ/			/leng+θ/
1	⇒	leŋg+θ	7	⇒	len+θ
7	⇒	[leŋθ]	1	⇒	[len̪θ]

(I am not concerned with the removal of the morpheme boundary.)

Table 6 presents the distribution of rules 7-12 in the six localities. Where rules 10, 11 and 12 are used only in the case of [ŋ], I have put an asterisk.

TABLE 6

S	SB	P	E	C	N
7	7	7	7(H)	7	7
8	8	10	10*	8	8
9(N) 9'(Y)	9''	11	11*	9	9
12	10	12	12*	10	10*
	11			11	11*
	12			12	12

Palatal harmony of /t/ and /d/ can be accounted for by rule 1 and the redundancy rules mentioned above which add [alv] and fricative release to palatal stops. Rule 13 accounts for palatal harmony in the case of /s/ and /z/.

13. [alv]   (opt.)
    [fric]
      ⇓
    [palatal] / ___ [palatal]

Some speakers block rule 13 and rule 1 from operating on /s/ and /z/, when [t] or [d] intervenes, i.e. *last chair* with CCS is [las tʃɛː] not [laʃ tʃɛː] (with different vowels as appropriate), and *Stuart* begins with [stʃ-] not [ʃtʃ-]. No speakers allow palatal harmony to apply to /t/ and /d/ before /tʃ/ or /dʒ/, thus *hot cheese* does not have [-tʃ tʃ-], and *glazed jars* does not have [-dʒ dʒ-]. After palatal harmony has occurred, the conditioning /j/ may be deleted if an unstressed vowel follows, as given in rule 14.

14. [liquid]   ⇒ ∅ / _____   V̌
    [palatal]   [palatal]

The derivation below is that of [kaʃe̥], Stockport (26).

/kasts jV̌/
7 ⇒ -ss j-
13 ⇒ -ʃʃ j-
12 ⇒ -ʃ j-
14 ⇒ [-ʃ]

There are cases where both rule 13 and CCS are involved and the latter is obligatory. For example, in *correction* CCS is obligatory, but not in *correct them*. It is not the intervening morpheme boundary that requires CCS, since in *lifts* and *costs*, for example, the /t/ can be retained. It is, rather, the combination of the palatal and the morpheme boundary that is crucial. We could, therefore, revise rule 7 as follows, giving one obligatory context and one optional one:

7. [αvoice] ⇒ ∅ / _____ { [palatal]⁺ } (obl.)
   [stop]   [αvoice] {   }
   [-nasal]   {   + C   } (opt.)

The morpheme boundary appears after the palatal consonant in the environment template to allow the rule to apply optionally to palatals derived by rule 13, as in *costs you* above (ie. *cost+s*). This means that the derivation of *correction* is as follows:

/kərekt+jən/
1 ⇒ -ktʃ+j-
14 ⇒ -ktʃ+-
7 ⇒ [-kʃ-]

Rule 14 is also obligatory in this context.

We must now return to /ð/, which I have dealt with under the general heading ð-harmony. /ð/ was given an unspecified manner feature above, because it is realized in a variety of ways, as we have seen in the individual chapters. In fact, we are dealing with two rules, plus rules 1 and 11. The redundancy rule 15 accounts for the contextual variants.

    15. If   [Ømanner]
                 [dental]
                   ⇓
        then [αmanner] / [αmanner] ____ (opt.)
                            [alv]
                   ⇓
     otherwise   [fric]

In the case of /-n ð-/ we have the following derivation:

           /n ð/
  1 ⇒   n̪ ð
 15 ⇒   n̪ d̪
 11 ⇒   n̪ n̪

in which all stages are possible surface versions. The output of rule 15 is more common in Coventry than in the other localities. In the case of /-l ð-/, /-z ð-/, /-s ð-/, /-(d)ʒ ð-/ and /-(t)ʃ ð-/, there is an optional change of [dental] to [alv], as in rule 16([13]).

    16. [dental] ⇒ [alv] / {[fric] } ____ (opt.)
                           {[liquid]} ([fric])
                           [alv]   ([liquid])

Thus:

         /l ð/   /z ð/   /tʃ ð/
 15 ⇒   l l̪   z ð   tʃ ð
 16 ⇒   l l   z z   tʃ z

(The first instance of [l] would, of course, be velarized.)

LENITION AND SYLLABLE STRUCTURE
As a final section to this chapter, I would like to take up some issues which point towards a non-linear approach to phonology, to which I have already alluded above in relation to glottal realization. In so doing, I hope to pick out areas for more

detailed investigation in the future.

In the Introduction I referred to a general schema for lenition as presented by Anderson and Ewen (1980: 28) and expanded by Ewen (1980: 175). Such phenomena as lenition are used by supporters of natural process phonology to argue against the SPE feature system which does not allow "strength scales" to be captured as unitary. Within the dependency framework proposed by Anderson and Ewen (1980) and Ewen (1980), lenition is seen as a gradual increase in the dominance and preponderance of the element |V| (= "relatively periodic") as opposed to |C| (which "correlates with the presence of zeros in the acoustic record of that segment") (cf. Anderson and Ewen, 1980: 25). These are components of the categorial gesture, the part of the phonological representation concerned with consonantality, voice, continuancy and sonorance (cf. Ewen, 1980: 134). Sequences of segment change in the history of various languages, such as:

$$x \longrightarrow \gamma \longrightarrow w \longrightarrow \emptyset$$

$$p \longrightarrow b \longrightarrow \beta$$

occurring in intervocalic position, are used as evidence for the establishment of such processes as natural and universal. (Child language acquisition phenomena are also cited as supportive evidence, e.g. Stampe, 1979, but see also Aitchison's caveat, 1981: 180-83.) However, there are other paths to deletion than the one exemplified above, and I would like to mention two here, one of which is particularly relevant to my data and does not seem at first sight to be related to lenition.

Both voiceless stops and voiceless fricatives disappear in circumstances other than intervocalically([14]), e.g.

Old Chinese γiep > Mandarin ɕiɛ;
compare Latin *septem* with Greek *hepta* > Modern Greek [ɛfta];
Latin *fumus* > Spanish *umo*.

We can see similar changes in English, both synchronically and diachronically, either in part or in toto. Consider glottal reinforcement in syllable-final position and the [ʔ] allophone of /t/ and /k/. Similarly, the voiceless velar fricative has disappeared from the English phoneme inventory:

ɛçtə > ɛɪçt > ɛɪht > ɛɪt

dɔxtər > dɔɯxtər > dɔɯhtər > dɔɯtər

(For a discussion of this process in more detail, see Lodge, ms.)

On the basis of this and similar evidence we can represent the deletion paths informally as follows:

p, t, k ⟶ ʔp, ʔt, ʔk ⟶ ʔ ⟶ ∅

f, s, θ, x ⟶ h ⟶ ∅

In both cases the process involves the loss of supraglottal stricture before the segment disappears altogether. The phase before deletion is simply [stop] and [-voice], respectively (cf. Lass, 1976: 163).

If we interpret this progression in terms of the activity of the vocal cords, we can see that all three types of deletion involve this aspect of articulation. In lenition we are dealing with vibrating vocal cords, with the stops with closed vocal cords, and with the fricatives with open vocal cords. If these are isolated separately as elements in the categorial gesture: |V|, |ʔ| and |O|, respectively, in a dependency notation, then we can explain the processes involved as loss of all the other phonological features before final deletion. (See Ewen, 1980, Lodge, 1981, and Davenport and Staun, ms, for arguments relating to the constituents in the categorial gesture.) Terms like "lenition" and "weakening" are not suitable for describing all three types of deletion path, especially as glottal reinforcement appears to be a "strengthening" of articulation, so I shall suggest the more general term "progressive feature loss" to cover all three.

We should perhaps enquire why some sounds seem to be subject to apparent strengthening processes when they are in an inherently weak syllable position. The notion of relatively strong and weak positions in the syllable has been developed by a number of phonologists (eg. Hooper, 1976, Foley, 1977, Liberman and Prince, 1977, Kiparsky, 1979, Selkirk, 1980, and Ewen, 1980) as an inherent property of phonological structure at various levels. Such strength hierarchies are related to sonority, the most sonorous sound being the strongest. In metrical phonology and dependency phonology the English word *pad* would be given the following syllable structures respectively:

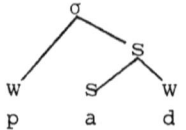 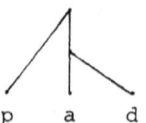

(cf. Kiparsky, 1979, and Anderson, ms.) In the dependency tree strength can be read off in terms of the nodes and the degrees of dependency(^{15}). In both representations syllable-initial position is weaker than nuclear position, but stronger than syllable-final position. In other accounts of syllable strength (eg. Hooper, 1976, and Foley, 1977) we find that syllable-initial position is characterised as strong. However, with the more subtle, relative strengths proposed by both metrical and dependency phonology, we can explain why weakening to zero is less common in initial position than in final position because the former is relatively stronger. If we accept the notion of relative strengths within the syllable, we can postulate processes which attempt to balance out the syllable values as well as reinforcing them(^{16}). That is why we find glottal reinforcement in English, an attempt to strengthen a weak syllable position. English is in a "strengthening phase" in this respect, in that it has glottal reinforcement in most accents, although there are signs of weakening in some accents, including those presented in this study, in that /p t k/ tend to be realized as [ʔ], the order of frequency being /t/, then /k/, then /p/ least often. Mandarin, on the other hand, has weakened the final stops to zero.

Another instance of strengthening a weak syllable position is devoicing of final voiced obstruents, complete in German and Russian, for instance, but only partial in English. We can find the alternation of strengthening and weakening in West Yorkshire voicing harmony (cf. Wells, 1982: 367, and Leslie, ms) in a word like *Bradford*, where /d/ being in syllable-final position is weaker than /f/ in the initial position of the following syllable. We can represent this informally, as follows:

where ⇐ = "strengthens to", and ⇒ = "weakens to".

In order to incorporate these aspects of lenition into our rules, we may wish to relate more closely rules which have so far been presented as separate. Let us take CCS and glottal reinforcement. The rules given above, 3 and 7, are quite distinct from one another. However, when we consider some of the sounds affected by them, namely /t/ and /k/, we could postulate the following progression as the deletion path related to glottal closure, as described above.

(i) Add glottal closure to all voiceless stops in context X.
(ii) Remove supraglottal closure from all glottally reinforced stops in context Y.
(iii) Remove glottal stop in context Z.

The first stage of the progression is captured by rule 3; the second and third stages by rules 4, 5 and 7. On the other hand, we can present stages (ii) and (iii) somewhat differently in rules 17 and 18.

17. [place] ⇒ ∅ / ___ (opt.)
    [glottal]
    [stop]

18. [glottal] ⇒ ∅ / ___ + C (obl.)
    [stop]   [-voice]

If rule 17 is chosen, rule 18 must be applied, since in the accents presented here with the exception of Norwich, forms such as *[pʌʊsʔmən] *postman* are not well-formed, whereas forms such as [sɔːɫʔmaɪn] *salt mine* are. This progression means that each glottal realization is generated via glottal reinforcement, and each deletion via both glottal reinforcement and glottal realization. The disadvantages of this approach are twofold: the glottal realization of /p t k/ has already been noted as being different in frequency for each of the stops, and this can only be accounted for by the optionality of rule 17; the deletion of /d/ under the same circumstances as /t/ has to be accounted for by a separate rule. It is, of course, true that in the case of /d/-deletion as determined by CCS, there is no evidence in the data presented here that we are dealing with a gradual deletion path, i.e. there are no instances of intermediate stages suggesting a path such as d ⟶ z ⟶ j ⟶ ∅. We, therefore, have to assume a "direct" deletion: d ⟶ ∅.

In the case of speaker Y /n/ displays the whole

range of a lenition path to deletion; the following are all realizations of /n/: [n], [ɨ̃], [ũ], [ɟ̃], [w̃], [ə̃], [ʌõ], [ø̃ʔ], ∅, the last two phonetic realizations being nasalization of part of the preceding vowel phase. These all occur in weak syllable position and the non-nasal features are determined by the following sound(s), i.e. [ɨ̃] occurs before /l/, [w̃] before ([ʔ])/w/, and so on([17]).

I have not gone into any detail regarding syllable structure, but have referred to the syllable throughout both informally and in the rules, e.g. rule 3. I have taken the view, supported by both metrical and dependency phonology, that the syllable is an appropriate level of phonological abstraction for the statement of certain regularities. Rule 3, for instance, would be more complicated without reference to the syllable boundary. We also have to refer to syllabification to account for the difference in the realization of /t/ in Stockport *cotton* versus *bottle*, for example. Furthermore, if we accept the notion of differential strength distributed in the syllable, some of the process rules can be formulated in terms of strength/weakness. We can explain why CCS operates in the way it does. Three consecutive weak positions reduce to two and it is the weakest position that is lost, e.g.

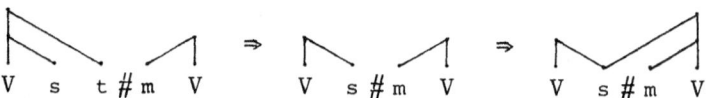

In the last stage there is resyllabification to produce overlap. On the other hand, in a CCV sequence the final weak C is strengthened by resyllabification making it ambisyllabic:

If such strength scales can be shown to be universal to natural languages, then considerable savings can be made in the grammars of individual languages. Their language-specific relevance is easier to demonstrate and it may well be that all the processes discussed in this study can be related to syllable structure and relative strength. That has yet to be demonstrated.

NOTES

1. Stampe's (1979: 32) point that where no alternation occurs [m] is different from [ŋ] in that the former is underlying but the latter is not, may be valid on psychological grounds, but he offers no support for his argument other than the spelling.

2. Further investigation of how children acquire their accents might give some indication as to what feature specifications are minimally necessary for the identification of utterances in that particular accent. It is quite clear, even on the basis of a small amount of evidence, that harmonized forms are learnt early, so that harmony, at least, constitutes an important part of the phonological system for the child as well as for the adult (cf. Lodge, 1983). Of course, Stampe (1979) would argue that all the child has to do is learn where to suppress such natural processes as harmony.

3. More investigation of lip-rounding in consonants is necessary to give a proper statement of this (cf. Brown's, 1981, discussion).

4. In the descriptions of the general phonetic characteristics of each accent I have used the terms *tense* and *lax* with reference to the musculature of the speech organs; these are not to be associated with the SPE features [+tense], [-tense].

5. Historically speaking, the modern English diphthongs come from different sources, either long vowels, as in *name*, or vowel + consonant, as in *day*. Although none of the accents presented here have this feature, several Northern accents still differentiate some instances of original long vowel and original vowel + consonant, as in *bite* with [aɪ] and *night* with [ɪi] (cf. Lodge, 1973). It may be that such a distinction should be made in the underlying segments of even RP, especially if we wish to account for the morphological alternations *right* - *righteous*, as opposed to *delight* - *delicious* (where the spelling of the noun is misleading), in the phonological component (see Lodge, ms).

6. I do not propose to offer any further support for such an analysis beyond the alternation criterion. However, there is some evidence from mis-spellings of unstressed vowels by both children and adults to suggest that we are not justified in assuming full vowels for all surface instances of [ə], since such an assumption is arbitrarily based on the standard orthography.

7. For arguments concerning syllable overlap and ambisyllabicity, see Anderson and Jones (1977: 94-112) and Ewen (1980: 180-84).

[8] In Leslie's discussion of glottal allophony (ms) he gives the rule of resyllabification as Left Capture, that is the segment in question loses its attachment to the underlying syllable to the right and is then "captured" by the syllable to the left. However, if the /t/ is made ambisyllabic in the underlying representation, the rule is one of releasing the right-hand dependency (Right Release), leaving only the left-hand one, as shown in the representations of *centre* above. In Leslie's data there are the negative items *bedtime* and *ragtime*. That these do not have glottal realization can be explained by the non-overlapping syllabification in the underlying form, ie.

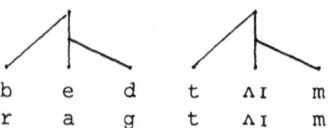

because English does not have any /-dt/ or /-gt/ clusters. *Sometime* [sʌmʔʌɪm] may be exceptional, though it depends whether *prompt* is /prɒmt/ or not. *Carlton* seems to be exceptional, too, with /-rlt/ in one syllable, but we must note that like all rhotic accents Edinburgh has final three-consonant clusters including /r/, eg. *world*, *words* and *pearls*.

[9]. The only other occurring sequences which fit the rule are /-lb/ in *bulb*, /-ldʒ/ in *bulge* and /-ndʒ/ in *change*. I have no evidence as to whether the /b/ would be deleted or not. In the plural form deletion would seem odd, but in rapid speech in an utterance such as *The bulb's gone* it might well take place. In my own rapid speech fricativization is more likely, i.e. [ðə bʌɬβz gɒn]. There is a tendency for the [d] to be deleted from /dʒ/, while the [ʒ] is retained, but again there are no instances in my recorded material.

[10]. With more data than I have used here it might be possible to show that certain processes are obligatory in certain styles, that is, equate the operation of particular rules with particular styles of delivery, interpreted by the native speaker as "formal", "casual", "posh", "common", and so on.

[11]. There are possible differences between informants C, B and W, which would involve adjustments to these rules in each case. Cf. Chapters 2 and 3, above.

[12]. I do not intend to pursue this point further here. For much fuller discussion of /ŋ/ in English

and German, see Goyvaerts (1978: 127-28) and Dressler (1981).

[13]. θ-harmony, as in *miss things* (cf. Lodge, 1981: 29), can be accounted for by rule 16, and θ-deletion, as in *sixth*, by applying Geminate Simplification afterwards. In *months* the order of the relevant segments is reversed and the rule would have to be revised to account for this too. NB: The examples containing [z] in Lodge (1981: 29-30) are incorrectly given a dental diacritic: [z̪].

[14]. For some interesting Celtic evidence, see Ó Dochartaigh (1980). For details of the change in Chinese, see Forrest (1973: 195).

[15]. I am not concerned here with whether we should take a metrical or a dependency view of syllable structure. Although there may be advantages to a dependency framework over a metrical one in terms of non-binarity and implicit strength values and structural levels that can be read off from the notation, I shall not attempt to argue the point here. On this and other matters, see Ewen (ms).

[16]. See Foley (1977: 123-26) for a discussion of "modular depotentiation" as his explanation for weakening of the strongest phonological elements. His treatment of English in this respect seems totally inadequate in terms of the data presented in this book.

[17]. For a discussion of /l/-deletion in Cockney and its relation to /r/-deletion, see Champ (1983). The former is not so widespread in the six accents discussed here as it is in Cockney.

REFERENCES

Aitchison, J. 1981. *Language change: progress or decay?* London: Fontana.

Aitken, A. J. 1962. Vowel length in Modern Scots. Mimeo: University of Edinburgh.

Anderson, J. M. ms. Suprasegmental structure. Paper presented at the Dependency Phonology Conference, University of Essex, 9-11 September 1983.

Anderson, J. M. and Ewen, C. J. 1980. *Studies in dependency phonology*. Ludwigsburg: Ludwigsburg Studies in Language and Linguistics 4.

Anderson, J. M. and Jones, C. 1977. *Phonological structure and the history of English*. Amsterdam: North-Holland.

Brown, G. 1972. *Phonological rules and dialect variation*. Cambridge: Cambridge University Press.

Brown, G. 1981. Consonant rounding in British English: the status of phonetic descriptions as historical data. In R. E. Asher and E. J. A. Henderson (eds.): *Towards a history of phonetics*. Edinburgh: Edinburgh University Press.

Champ, P. 1983. The evaporation of liquids in Cockney. *Nottingham Linguistic Circular*. 12.1: 1-20.

Cheshire, J. 1982. Linguistic variation and social function. In Romaine (1982).

Chomsky, A. N. 1980. *Rules and representations*. Oxford: Basil Blackwell.

Chomsky, A. N. and Halle, M. 1968. *The sound pattern of English*. New York: Harper and Row. (= SPE)

Cutler, A. 1980. Productivity in word formation. *CLS*. 16: 45-51.

Davenport, M. and Staun, J. ms. Some problems for dependency phonology. Paper presented at the Dependency Phonology Conference, University of Essex, 9-11 September 1983.

Dorian, N. C. 1982. Defining the speech community to include its working margins. In Romaine (1982).

Dresher, B. E. 1981. Abstractness and explanation in phonology. In N. Hornstein and D. Lightfoot (eds.): *Explanation in linguistics*. London: Longman.

Dressler, W. U. 1975. Methodisches zu Allegro-Regeln. In W. U. Dressler and F. V. Mareš (eds.): *Phonologica 1972*. Munich: Wilhelm Fink.

Dressler, W. U. 1981. External evidence for an

abstract analysis of the German velar nasal. In D. L. Goyvaerts (ed.): Phonology in the 1980s. Ghent: E. Story-Scientia.

Ewen, C. J. 1977. Aitken's law and the phonatory gesture in dependency phonology. Lingua. 41: 307-29.

Ewen, C. J. 1980. Aspects of phonological structure. Unpublished doctoral thesis, University of Edinburgh.

Ewen, C. J. ms. Segmental structure. Paper presented at the Dependency Phonology Conference, University of Essex, 9-11 September 1983.

Ferguson, C. 1978. Phonological processes. In J. H. Greenberg et al. (eds.): Universals of human language. Stanford: Stanford University Press.

Foley, J. 1970. Phonological distinctive features. Folia Linguistica. 4: 87-92.

Foley, J. 1977. Foundations of theoretical phonology. Cambridge: Cambridge University Press.

Forrest, R. A. D. 1973. The Chinese language. (3rd ed.) London: Faber and Faber.

Fudge, E. C. 1967. The nature of phonological primes. JL. 3: 1-36.

Fudge, E. C. 1969a. Mutation rules and ordering in phonology. JL. 5: 23-38.

Fudge, E. C. 1969b. Syllables. JL. 5: 253-86.

Giles, H. and Powesland, P. F. 1975. Speech style and social evaluation. London and New York: Academic Press.

Gimson, A. C. 1962. An introduction to the pronunciation of English. London: Edward Arnold.

Goldsmith, J. 1976a. Autosegmental phonology. Bloomington: Indiana University Linguistics Club.

Goldsmith, J. 1976b. An overview of autosegmental phonology. LA. 2: 23-68.

Goyvaerts, D. L. 1978. Aspects of post-SPE phonology. Ghent: E. Story-Scientia.

Guy, G. 1980. Variation in the group and the individual: the case of final stop deletion. In Labov (1980).

Hardcastle, W. J. 1981. Experimental studies in lingual coarticulation. In R. E. Asher and E. J. A. Henderson (eds.): Towards a history of phonetics. Edinburgh: Edinburgh University Press.

Hasegawa, N. 1979. Casual speech vs. fast speech. CLS. 15: 126-37.

Hockett, C. F. 1958. A course in modern linguistics. New York: Macmillan.

Hooper, J. B. 1976. An introduction to natural

generative phonology. New York: Academic Press.
Hughes, A. and Trudgill, P. J. 1979. <u>English accents and dialects</u>. London: Edward Arnold.
Hyman, L. M. 1975. <u>Phonology: theory and analysis</u>. New York: Holt, Rinehart and Winston.
Kiparsky, P. 1968. <u>How abstract is phonology?</u> Bloomington: Indiana University Linguistics Club.
Kiparsky, P. 1979. Metrical structure assignment is cyclic. <u>LI</u>. 10: 421-41.
Knowles, G. 1978. The nature of phonological variables in Scouse. In Trudgill (1978).
Labov, W. 1980. The social origins of sound change. In W. Labov (ed.): <u>Locating language in time and space</u>. New York: Academic Press.
Ladefoged, P. 1982. <u>A course in phonetics</u>. (2nd ed.) New York: Harcourt, Brace and Jovanovich.
Lass, R. 1976. <u>English phonology and phonological theory</u>. Cambridge: Cambridge University Press.
Leslie, D. ms. Left capture and British voiceless stop allophony. Paper presented at the XIX Congress of the International Association of Logopaedics and Phoniatrics, University of Edinburgh, 14-18 August 1983.
Liberman, M. and Prince, A. 1977. On stress and linguistic rhythm. <u>LI</u>. 8: 249-336.
Lodge, K. R. 1966. The Stockport dialect. <u>Le maître phonétique</u>. 126: 26-30.
Lodge, K. R. 1973. Stockport revisited. <u>JIPA</u>. 3: 81-87.
Lodge, K. R. 1976. Some arguments concerning idealization in linguistic descriptions. <u>University of East Anglia Papers in Linguistics</u>. 1: 1-14.
Lodge, K. R. 1978. A Stockport teenager. <u>JIPA</u>. 8: 56-71.
Lodge, K. R. 1979. A three-dimensional analysis of non-standard English. <u>Journal of Pragmatics</u>. 3: 169-195.
Lodge, K. R. 1931. Dependency phonology and English consonants. <u>Lingua</u>. 54: 19-39.
Lodge, K. R. 1983. The acquisition of phonology: a Stockport sample. <u>Lingua</u>.
Lodge, K. R. ms. The English velar fricative, dialect variation and dependency phonology. Paper presented at the Dependency Phonology Conference, University of Essex, 9-11 September 1983.
Lodge, K. R. In preparation. Testing native speaker predictions of variant forms of English.
Lyons, J. 1962. Phonemic and non-phonemic phonology: some typological reflections. <u>IJAL</u>. 28: 131-58.

McEntegart, D. and Le Page, R. B. 1982. An appraisal of the statistical techniques used in the Sociolinguistic Survey of Multilingual Communities. In Romaine (1982).
Milroy, J. 1982. The tip of the iceberg. In Romaine (1982).
Milroy, J. and Milroy, L. 1978. Belfast: change and variation in an urban vernacular. In Trudgill (1978).
Milroy, L. 1980. Language and social networks. Oxford: Basil Blackwell.
Neu, H. 1980. Ranking of constraints on /t, d/ deletion in American English: a statistical analysis. In Labov (1980).
Newton, B. 1970. Cypriot Greek, its phonology and inflections. The Hague: Mouton.
Ó Dochartaigh, C. 1980. Aspects of Celtic lenition. In Anderson and Ewen (1980).
Orton, H. et al. (eds.) 1962-71. Survey of English Dialects, Volumes I-IV. Leeds: Arnold. (= SED)
Palmer, F. R. (ed.) 1970. Prosodic analysis. London: Oxford University Press.
Petyt, K. M. 1978. Secondary contractions in West Yorkshire negatives. In Trudgill (1978).
Petyt, K. M. 1980. The study of dialect. London: André Deutsch.
Romaine, S. 1978. Postvocalic /r/ in Scottish English: sound change in progress? In Trudgill (1978).
Romaine, S. (ed.) 1982. Sociolinguistic variation in speech communities. London: Edward Arnold.
Sankoff, D. (ed.) 1978. Linguistic variation: models and methods. New York: Academic Press.
Selkirk, E. O. 1980. The role of prosodic categories in English word stress. LI. 11: 563-605.
Stampe, D. 1979. A dissertation on natural phonology. Including: The acquisition of phonetic representation. Bloomington: Indiana University Linguistics Club.
Strang, B. M. H. 1970. A history of English. London: Methuen.
Tiersma, P. 1983. The nature of phonological representation: evidence from breaking in Frisian. JL. 19: 59-78.
Trager, G. L. and Smith H. L. 1951. An outline of English structure. Studies in Linguistics, Occasional Papers, 3. Norman, Oklahoma: Battenburg Press.
Trudgill, P. J. 1974. The social differentiation of English in Norwich. Cambridge: Cambridge University Press.

Trudgill, P. J. 1978. Sociolinguistic patterns in British English. London: Edward Arnold.
Trudgill, P. J. 1980/83. Acts of conflicting identity. In Trudgill (1983).
Trudgill, P. J. 1983. On dialect. Oxford: Basil Blackwell.
Trudgill, P. J. 1983a. Sociolinguistics and linguistic theory. In Trudgill (1983).
Trudgill, P. J. and Foxcroft, T. 1978. On the sociolinguistics of vocalic mergers: transfer and approximation in East Anglia. In Trudgill (1978).
Vihman, M. M. 1978. Consonant harmony: its scope and function in child language. In J. H. Greenberg et al. (eds.) Universals of human language. Stanford: Stanford University Press.
Wells, J. C. 1982. Accents of English, Volumes 1 and 2. Cambridge: Cambridge University Press.
Zwicky, A. 1972. Casual speech. CLS. 8: 607-15.

INDEX

abstractness 4, 5
acquisition (child language) 5, 7, 16-17, 44-45, 142, 147
affricate 125
Aitken's Law 93
allegro rules 2, 21
ambisyllabicity see syllable overlap
approximant 125-126
(Ancient) Greek 142
Anderson & Ewen 3, 5, 6, 142
assimilation see harmony

biuniqueness 4

categorial gesture 142-143
Celtic 149
Chomsky & Halle (SPE) 2, 3, 4, 19, 40, 61, 121, 127-128, 142, 147
Cockney 51, 149
colloquial speech 1, 2, 5, 10, 123
competence 1, 2, 4, 17, 19
concreteness 5 see also natural phonology
Consonant Cluster Simplification (CCS) 5, 9-10, 24, 38, 40-41, 43, 46-48, 57, 59, 60-62, 77-78, 92, 104-105, 107, 117-118, 136-137, 140, 145, 146
Coventry 10, 13, 95-107, 137, 141
creaky voice 29, 51, 108

deletion 9-10, 142-146, 148
/g/ 47, 50, 61, 78, 92, 105, 138-139
/j/ 48, 140
/r/ 12-13, 62, 73-74, 78, 93-94, 149
unstressed vowel (UVD) 10-11, 12, 14, 39, 40-41, 48-49, 60, 62, 78, 92-93, 105-106, 107, 118-119, 134, 135
denasalization 95
dependency phonology 3, 10, 24, 132, 134, 142-146, 149
devoicing 74, 90-91, 104, 144
diphthong 49, 50, 89, 127-128, 147
distinctive features 121-128, 147

Edinburgh 10, 11, 80-94, 123, 124, 126, 127, 128, 134, 136, 137
epenthesis 41, 62, 118
Ewe 121
/ə/ 128-129, 147

flap 49, 58, 72, 80, 89, 102, 106, 108, 116

155

Geminate Simplification (GS) 48, 59, 60, 61, 73, 75-76, 104-105, 106-107, 116, 118, 137, 138-139, 149
German 144
glide 127
glottal reinforcement 22, 39, 108, 123, 131-132, 133-134, 142-143, 144, 145
glottal stop 16, 21-23, 39-42, 49, 78, 89, 102, 108, 116, 118, 119, 123, 132-136, 142, 144, 145, 148

/h/ 38, 57, 72, 89, 102, 116, 129, 131
harmony 7-9, 42-46, 57, 58-60, 61, 64, 74-77, 91-92, 103-104, 116-117, 123, 124, 125, 129, 131, 138-139, 147
  consonantal 5, 7, 39, 42-46, 58-60, 61, 74-77, 91-92, 103-104, 116-117, 125, 131
  left-to-right 8, 58, 61, 75-76, 138-139, 141
  manner 8, 45, 58, 60, 75-77, 91-92, 103-104, 106-107, 125, 141
  nasal 10, 46, 58-59, 61, 104, 106, 117, 137, 138-139, 141
  palatal 2, 8, 43-44, 59, 77, 92, 103, 117, 125, 139
  place 7-8, 42-43, 46-48, 58, 60, 61, 74-75, 90-91, 103-104, 106-107, 116-117, 137
  voice 5, 8-9, 77, 138, 144
hypercorrection 25
hyperdialectalism 25

language and society 20-24
Latin 142
Latinate vocabulary 3-5, 24

lenition 6, 9, 42, 45, 57-58, 72-74, 89-90, 102, 116, 138, 141-146
lexical entry 3, 121, 123, 128, 135
lexical incidence 129, 130-131
lip position 29-30, 32, 38, 51, 53, 64, 78, 81, 95, 108, 126, 147
liquid 125-126, 137
Liverpool 95
/l/-vocalization 42, 46, 57, 60, 73, 80, 89, 102

Mandarin 123, 142, 144
Maori 123
metrical phonology 143-144, 146, 149
Middle English 19, 128
Modern Greek 123, 142
morpheme boundary 10, 61, 137, 139, 140
morphological alternations 3-5, 12, 24, 121-122, 139, 147

nasalization see harmony, nasal
natural phonology 142
Norwich 13, 17, 20, 50, 108-120, 127, 128, 132, 134, 136, 145
[ŋ] 38, 46-47, 57, 61-62, 72, 78, 92, 102, 105, 116, 131, 137, 138-139, 147, 148-149

Old Chinese 142

panlectal grammars 14-18
Peasmarsh 5, 6-12, 64-79, 104, 105, 118, 137, 138
phonology 3-14, 121-149
polylectal grammars 14-18, 24
process(es) 1-14, 123, 129, 131-149
progressive feature loss 123, 143

/r/ 12-14, 29, 39, 57, 64, 72, 73-74, 75, 77, 80, 89-91, 102, 106, 108, 116, 118, 119, 125-126, 131, 137, 148
  linking 12-14, 49, 62, 90, 106, 118, 119, 129
realization rules 12-13, 123
redundancy rules 121, 124-125, 126, 129, 131, 139, 141
Right Release (RR) 136, 148
RP 10, 14-15, 17, 18, 23, 81, 91, 93, 115, 120, 127, 129, 147
Russian 144

SED 40, 50
segment 3, 129, 142, 147, 148, 149
Shepherd's Bush 6-12, 51-63, 78, 105, 137, 138
sociolinguistics see language and society
sonority 143
Spanish 142
Stampe 2, 3, 5, 7, 44, 142, 147
Stockport 5, 6-12, 17-18, 19-20, 21-23, 24-25, 29-50, 57, 78, 95, 102, 118, 134-135, 136, 137, 138, 140, 146
stress placement rule 14, 40-41, 60, 106-107, 119, 128, 135
style 1, 5, 21, 148
syllable boundary 48, 132, 146
syllable overlap 132-134, 136, 146, 147, 148
syllable structure 47, 132-136, 141-146, 148
systematic phonemic level 3, 121-123

tenseness 127, 147
Thai 123
trisyllabic laxing 4

Trudgill 1, 5, 9, 12, 13, 16, 17, 18, 20, 21, 24, 25, 108, 115, 116, 118, 128

Ulster 80

voicing 58, 61, 116
  see also lenition
vowel length 127-128
vowel lengthening 62-63, 79, 93-94, 106, 119-120

Wells 1, 9, 12, 13, 51, 61, 62, 80, 81, 89, 93, 102, 108, 144
West Yorkshire 9, 144
word-boundary 2, 8, 11, 48, 118
/ʍ/ 89

/x/ 89, 142-143

WORD INDEX

The word index contains forms which are discussed phonetically and/or phonologically in the text of the book. It does not contain references to the transcriptions, nor forms from the indented lists of examples in the various chapters. With four exceptions there are only one-word entries.

about 102, 128
across 117
afternoon 133, 134
air 115
alright 38
always 89, 117
asked 10, 104

band 79
battery 49
better 39, 133, 136
birds 90
bite 147
blond 63
boat 130
book 16, 130
born 90
bother 104
bottom 6
Bradford 144
breakfast 120
butcher 15, 23
by 89

can't 38, 61
car 12, 131
cart 130, 131
carter 131
centre 133, 134
church 12, 130
city 132, 136
clash 115
cleared 115
come 15, 23
comfortable 11
coming 46

company 92
correction 140
cottages 72
cotton 133
country 117
court 90
cure 118

divine 4
divinity 4, 19
done 29, 63
don't 61
door 12
down 79
-dung 105
during 90

Edinburgh 81, 90, 91
eighty 81
electric 3
electricity 3
end 76
England 91
English 47
eruption 117
eye 38

fade 3, 4
farm 12
father 19
fed 4
fin 4
fine 4
first 90, 133
from 91
fur 12

getting 102
glisten 6
go 115
gone 79
got 39, 119
got a 29, 132-133, 136
grind 76

half 21-22
handkerchief 6
Harriet's 115
heel 115
her 115
here 115
high 89
him 117
hit 133

I 89
-ing 46-48, 50, 61, 78, 92
inside 89
inverted 115
issue 8
it's 39

labourer 11
lamb 61
lane 115
lantern 79
last 6, 119, 130
law of 12-13
left 108
Leith 92
length 139
letter 12-13, 29
like 39, 60, 116
listen 6
little 108
look 16, 108
lost 133
lot (of) 72, 93

markedly 91
materials 115
merchant 90
more 130

nature 8
nicked 39
night 20, 23, 147
no 115

nobody 92
nothing 105

off 79, 119
older 89, 90
or 90
otherwise 90
outside 89

pad 143-144
park 90
pavement 59
people 6, 89
Pepper's 29
perplex 12
photograph 128
picture 133
planting 106
pleasure 2
plenty 118
port 12
posher 90
Protestant 89
put 115

quarter of 14

rattles 39
recognize 89
red 4
reed 4
reflection 117
right 20, 38, 147
righteous 19, 147

same 115
sandbag 103
sand-castle 5-6
school 89, 115
Scotland 133
secondary 92
seemed 59
send 63, 138
serene 3
serenity 3
serve 130
served 90
shame 79
short 90
shoulder 115
sing 61, 138-139

something 46, 59, 61-62, 137
sort 130
staithe 115
stopped 116
style 6
sugar 8
suit 8

take 3
tall 130
telegram 63
that 63, 116, 119
the 39-42, 134-136
them 117
then 137
there 115
think 79, 91, 116, 138
thing(s) 47, 137
third 90
three 39, 115
through 115
time 38
to 116, 134-136
took 3, 116
trace 91
tuning 105
turns 137

up 79
upholsterer 49

very 14, 75

waiting 39
want 137
wanted 59
was 78
wasn't 49
went 133, 138
when 89
wonder 61
work 91

year 90, 115

For Product Safety Concerns and Information please contact our EU
representative GPSR@taylorandfrancis.com
Taylor & Francis Verlag GmbH, Kaufingerstraße 24, 80331 München, Germany

www.ingramcontent.com/pod-product-compliance
Lightning Source LLC
Chambersburg PA
CBHW070402240426
43661CB00056B/2510